THE KITCHEN
COMPANION

Photography
Cut-out photographs: Paul Turner and
    Sue Pressley, Stonecastle Graphics Ltd,
    Marden, Kent, England
Recipe photographs: Colour Library Books

Design
Paul Turner and Sue Pressley,
Stonecastle Graphics Ltd

Editorial
Compiled and edited: Wendy Hobson

Jacket Design
Zapp

Published in 1993 by
Tormont Publications Inc.
338 Saint Antoine St. East
Montreal, Canada, H2Y 1A3
Tel. (514) 954-1441
Fax (514) 954-1443

ISBN 2-89429-327-5

Printed in U.S.A.

THE KITCHEN COMPANION

Your Seasonal Guide to Delicious Recipes

Compiled and edited by Wendy Hobson

TORMONT

Making the Most of the Seasons

EVERY SEASON and every month of the year has its own special associations: from the rich and warming soups which ward off the cold of a January day to the luscious soft fruits of summer, the crisp russet apples of autumn, and all the traditional delights of the Christmas season.

The Kitchen Companion contains a seasonal selection of recipes, hints and tips to help you make the best of foods in season and create tasty dishes all the year round. Of course, you do not have to restrict yourself to making the dishes just at one particular time of the year, for you are sure to find favorites you will want to cook again and again.

Many foods are now available in the supermarket throughout the year, and are often of excellent quality, even when out of season. But they can be more expensive so watch out for both price and quality. It is often the best idea to use foods when they are in season, particularly fruits and vegetables. Not only are they cheapest at that time, the flavor will be at its best. You may be able to buy lovely-looking Brussels sprouts in March, but the taste could be bitter and will not compare with the sweet, nutty sprouts you can buy at Christmas. Tomatoes are available all the year round, but you will find the tastiest, juiciest ones are those which have ripened under a summer sun. And with every month offering you a different selection of produce, there is always something to look forward to.

Try to use fresh produce where possible. It will not only taste the best, but is also the best for you, as it will contain its full complement of vitamins and minerals. Avoid buying foods which look faded or tired; they are past their best.

If you are short of time to prepare fresh foods or want to use produce out of season, look for canned or frozen varieties, many of which offer excellent value and quality. Keep a basic store cupboard so that you can always put together something interesting at short notice.

Many of the recipes in this book are simple and quick to prepare, so they are ideal for the busy household where you need a tasty and nutritious meal without complicated preparation or long cooking times.

All the recipes are simply presented so you can see at a glance what you need and how to prepare it. There are many suggestions for variations to recipes, and you can always experiment to make your own versions of the dishes. If you do not have a particular ingredient, just look through the recipe and see whether you can leave it out, or substitute something else you have in the cupboard. Never be afraid to try out new ideas of your own, especially using foods which you have grown yourself, which are in season or readily available.

You will not need any special kitchen equipment. Of course, if you have a food processor, blender or mixer, do use them to speed up slicing, chopping, blending or any other preparation.

Cooking Tips

THESE HANDY tips will help you make the best use of your *Kitchen Companion*.

1   Store foods carefully to maintain their freshness. Always remove plastic wrappings as they will cause foods to sweat. Store fruits and vegetables on a cool shelf or at the bottom of the refrigerator. Wrap cheese or cooked meats in foil and store in the refrigerator, removing cheese 1 hour before serving to allow it to ripen. Place raw meats on a plate, cover well and make sure they do not come into contact with other foods in the refrigerator.

2   Watch for best-before dates when you are shopping and use up fresh foods by the date indicated.

3   Always wash fresh produce before preparation.

4   Eggs in these recipes are 2-ounce or large eggs. If you do not have large eggs, simply add a little more or less water to the mixture to obtain the desired consistency.

5   Follow one set of measurements only. Do not mix volume (cup) and weight measurements.

6   Spoon measurements are level. It is best to use a set of measuring spoons as they are accurate and easy to use. Spoons meant for serving food vary in size depending on the design.

7   Adjust seasonings and strongly flavored ingredients, such as onions and garlic, to suit your own taste. If you are not keen on a particularly strong spice or flavoring, leave it out or substitute something else.

8   Use fresh herbs where possible as they will give you the best flavor and texture. There are only a few exceptions, such as oregano, the flavor of which develops when it is properly dried. If you do substitute dried for fresh herbs, use only half the amount specified. Do not use dried herbs for garnish or add them at the end of a recipe, as they will taste raw.

9   Always use freshly ground black pepper for seasoning. If you do not use salt in your cooking, you may want to add a few additional herbs.

10   For convenience, the recipes list butter, but you can substitute margarine if you prefer.

11   If you do not have the particular cooking pot called for in the recipe, look at the photograph and select the most suitable item you have.

12   Cooking temperatures are given for Fahrenheit and Celsius. Because ovens vary, times are approximate and may need to be adjusted to suit your oven. Convection ovens, for example, will require lower temperatures and the food will take less time to cook. You know your own oven best, so adjust times and temperatures as necessary.

13   All the recipes serve 4 unless otherwise stated.

Kitchen Store Cupboard

A WELL-STOCKED cupboard means you can always prepare a simple but tasty meal even at those times when you need to put together something from nothing! Use these suggestions to give you more ideas.

Bottles and jars: honey, jam, oil, syrup.
Cans: different kinds of beans, corned beef, fruits in natural juice, salmon, tuna.
Dry goods: baking powder, baking soda, cocoa powder, custard powder, flour, oatmeal, pasta, rice, stock cubes, sugar.
Frozen goods: bread, cream, filo pastry, fish fillets, shrimp, puff pastry.
Fruits and nuts: almonds, ground almonds, dried fruits, walnuts.

Herbs and spices: cayenne pepper, cinnamon, curry powder, nutmeg, oregano, mixed herbs, parsley, pepper, salt.
Miscellaneous: butter, eggs, long-life or evaporated milk.
Sauces: tomato paste, Worcestershire sauce.
Vegetables: carrots, onions, potatoes.

Bean Salad: Drain, rinse and mix a selection of canned beans. Dress with French dressing (see page 8) and sprinkle with fresh herbs.

Fish Sticks: Coat strips of fish fillet in egg and flour and fry in butter or oil. Serve with a white sauce (see page 8) flavored with chopped fresh or dried parsley, potatoes and peas.

Shrimp Parcels: Make a thick white sauce (see page 8) using half milk and half chicken stock, and stir in some shrimp. Use to fill little parcels made of layers of filo pastry brushed with oil and twisted together at the top. Brush with oil and bake in a preheated oven at 400°F (200°C) for 6 to 10 minutes.

Corned Beef Fritters: Coat cubes of corned beef in a thick batter (see page 8) and fry until golden.

Tuna Quiche: Line a quiche pan with shortcrust pastry (see page 8), spread with drained tuna and season with salt, pepper and cayenne pepper. Beat 2 eggs with ½ cup (125 ml) cream or milk, pour over the tuna and bake in a preheated oven at 400°F (200°C) for 30 minutes.

Pasta Bowl: Mix cooked pasta with a selection of beans, chopped onion, shrimp or chopped corned beef. Mix with mayonnaise (see page 8) flavored with tomato purée or curry powder.

Tasty Trifle: Layer sponge cake or fingers and drained canned fruit in a bowl and use the juice to make a jelly. Spoon the jelly over the fruit and leave to set. Top with custard and decorate with grated chocolate.

Chocolate Cake: Beat together ⅔ cup (150 ml) milk, ⅔ cup (150 ml) vegetable oil, 2 eggs, 2 tbsp corn syrup, 1¾ cup (200 g) all-purpose flour, ¾ cup (150 g) granulated sugar, 2 tbsp cocoa powder, 1 tsp baking soda. Bake in 2 greased and lined 7 inch (18 cm) cake pans in a preheated 325°F (160°C) oven for 35 minutes. Sandwich together with whipped cream.

Basic Recipes

Stock

1 chicken carcass, meat
   bones, or fish heads,
   bones and skin

1 onion
1 carrot
1 stick celery

Place the meat or fish in a saucepan with a selection of vegetables to give the stock flavor. Just cover with cold water, bring slowly to the boil and simmer for 1½ hours. Strain, then return the stock to the pan and boil to reduce the liquid. Use quickly or freeze.

Batter

1 cup (100 g) all-purpose
   flour
a pinch of salt

1 egg
⅔ cup (150 ml) milk

Beat all the ingredients together until the batter is smooth. Alter the amount of milk to adjust the consistency of the batter.

White Sauce

2 tbsp butter
4 tbsp flour

1¼ cups (300 ml) milk

Melt the butter, stir in the flour and cook for 1 minute. Whisk in the milk and bring to a boil, stirring continuously until the sauce thickens. Alter the amount of milk used to thicken or thin the sauce.

French Dressing

8 tbsp oil
4 tbsp wine vinegar
2 tsp Dijon mustard
salt and pepper

Shake all the
ingredients
together well in
a screw-top jar.

Mayonnaise

1 egg
1 egg yolk
½ tsp salt
½ tsp dry mustard

2 tbsp lemon juice
1 tbsp white wine vinegar
1½ cups (375 ml) oil

Place all the ingredients except the oil in a blender and mix well. Add one-third of the oil and mix again. With the blender running, gradually pour in the remaining oil until the mayonnaise thickens. Flavor, if desired, with spices, herbs or tomato purée.

Basic Bread

3 lb (1.5 kg) all-purpose
   flour
2 tbsp salt

1 tbsp quick-acting dry yeast
2 tbsp (25 g) shortening
3⅔ cups (900 ml) warm water

Mix together the flour, salt, yeast and shortening in a food processor. With the motor running, gradually pour in the water until the mixture forms a dough. Process until smooth and elastic and no longer sticky. Cover and let rise for 2 hours. Knead again, place in greased loaf tins, cover and leave to rise for a further 1 hour before baking at 450° F (230° C) for 40 minutes.

Shortcrust Pastry

2 cups (225 g) all-purpose
   flour
a pinch of salt

4 tbsp butter
4 tbsp lard
3 tbsp water

Sift the flour and salt. Rub in the butter and lard until the mixture resembles breadcrumbs. Mix in enough water to make a soft pastry. Do not overwork. Use as directed in the recipe.

Cooking for Children

MOST CHILDREN love cooking, and they can have great fun in a well-supervised kitchen making meals for their friends or for the family. Always remember that safety comes first. Teach children to be careful of sharp knives and graters, hot pans, food, foil, ovens and steam. Always supervise children while they are cooking.

Sausage Casserole

1 lb (450 g) sausage meat
2 tbsp all-purpose flour
salt and pepper
1 cooking apple, peeled,
    cored and sliced
1 onion, sliced
½ tsp dried mixed herbs
14 oz (400 g) canned
    tomatoes

Divide the sausage meat into 16 equal balls. Sprinkle the flour with salt and pepper and roll the balls in the flour. Place the apple, onion and sausage balls in an ovenproof dish. Sprinkle with herbs and pour the tomatoes on top. Sprinkle with salt and pepper. Cover and cook in a preheated oven at 350° F (180° C) for 1 hour. Serve with mashed potatoes and peas.

Baked Cheese Fingers

8 large slices brown bread
2 tbsp butter
4 slices cheese
1 egg, beaten
⅔ cup (150 ml) milk
salt and pepper

Remove the crusts from the bread and spread each slice with butter. Cover 4 pieces of bread with cheese and top with the remaining bread. Cut each sandwich into 3 fingers. Mix the egg and milk and sprinkle with salt and pepper. Dip the sandwiches in the milk mixture and arrange in a shallow ovenproof dish. Pour any remaining egg mixture on top. Bake in a preheated oven at 350° F (180° C) for 15 minutes. Serve with salad.

Potato Surprises

4 baking potatoes, scrubbed
2 tbsp butter
2 tbsp milk
2 oz (50 g) cheese, grated
4 eggs

Cut a cross through the skins of the potatoes and bake in a preheated oven at 400° F (200° C) for 1 hour until soft. Cool. Scoop out the potatoes into a bowl and mash with the butter, milk and cheese. Half-fill each potato skin with the cheese mixture. Break an egg into each one. Cover with the remaining cheese mixture. Place on middle rack of oven and brown under the broiler.

Hot Ham Crusties

4 bread rolls
6 tbsp soft margarine
grated rind of ½ orange
1 tsp chopped fresh parsley
¼ lb (100 g) ham, chopped
salt and pepper

Cut a thin slice off the top of each roll. Carefully pull out the centre and crumble into breadcrumbs. Mix the breadcrumbs with all the other ingredients and spoon back into the rolls. Replace the tops and wrap each roll completely in foil. Place on a baking pan and bake in a preheated oven at 375° F (190° C) for 20 minutes. Serve hot.

Macaroons

⅔ cup (150 ml) sweetened
    condensed milk
3 tbsp cocoa powder
2½ cups (375 ml)
    grated coconut
¼ tsp vanilla extract
a pinch of salt
a pinch of ground cloves

Mix thoroughly the milk, cocoa powder, coconut, vanilla, salt and cloves. Drop by spoonfuls onto a greased cookie sheet. Leave 2 inch (5 cm) spaces between each macaroon. Bake for 15 minutes in a preheated 350° F (180° C) oven.

Fairy Cakes

⅞ cup (200 g) soft margarine
⅔ cup (4 oz) sugar
1 cup (100 g) all-purpose flour
1 tsp baking powder
2 eggs
2 cups (160 g) icing sugar
24 jelly beans

Mix together 8 tbsp of the margarine with the sugar, flour, baking powder and eggs until smooth and soft. Spoon the mixture into paper liners in muffin tins and bake in a preheated 350° F (180° C) for about 15 minutes. Place the remaining margarine in a bowl an sift in the icing sugar. Mix together to form icing. (You can color this with a few drops of food coloring if you wish.) Spread a little on the top of each cooled cake and top with a jelly bean.

January

'January brings the snow,
Makes our feet and fingers glow.'
Anon

CHRISTMAS is over and the New Year begins with resolutions – will we keep them this year? With cold winds and winter snows covering the ground, the comfort of the kitchen offers rich and warming winter soups and stews, mellowed with a spoonful of sherry or wine. The best meals for these cold days are filling and satisfying to banish the winter chills. Days are at their shortest now and evenings are the time to enjoy the coziness of home.

JANUARY

1 New Year's Day

5 Make a winter vegetable soup with chicken stock and your favorite vegetables. Purée for a thick soup, then stir in a spoonful of cream.

2 Resolve to try some different cheeses this year: Danish Mycella, Italian Dolcelatte and French Roquefort are all delicious.

6 Twelfth Night

3

7

4 Seville marmalade oranges are available. Squeeze the juice from 3 lb (1.5 kg) oranges and 2 lemons. Tie the seeds in cheesecloth. Soak the chopped peel overnight in 16 cups (4 liters) water. Add the seeds and juice and simmer for 1 ½ hours until the peel is soft. Discard the seeds, stir in 3 lb (1.5 kg) sugar and boil for 20 minutes until set.

Onion Soup

2 lb (900 g) onions, sliced
2 tsp sugar
¼ cup (50 g) margarine
½ cup (50 g) all-purpose flour
6 cups (1.5 l) chicken or
  vegetable stock
½ cup (125 ml) dry white wine

1 tsp dried thyme
salt and pepper
12 slices French bread
2 tbsp olive oil
1 oz (25 g) Cheddar cheese,
  grated
fresh parsley for garnish

Brown the onions and sugar gently in the margarine for 15 minutes, stirring occasionally. Stir in the flour and cook for 1 minute. Gradually stir in the stock, wine and seasonings. Partially cover and simmer for 30 minutes.

Lightly brush both sides of the bread slices with the oil and broil one side until pale golden. Turn the bread over, sprinkle with the cheese and broil until golden brown. Serve the soup in individual bowls with the bread slices floating on top. Garnish with fresh parsley.

Brushing the bread with olive oil makes it wonderfully crisp when toasted under a hot broiler, giving a good contrast to the smooth soup. Try any hard cheese of your choice for the croutons: Gruyère and Parmesan impart wonderful strong flavors.

8

12

Lay pork chops on a bed of sliced apples, onions and mushrooms, pour on some apple juice, top with breadcrumbs and cheese and bake for 40 minutes.

9

For Duchesse Potatoes, beat 1 egg into mashed potatoes, pipe into swirls and bake at 400°F (200°C) for 30 minutes.

13

10

14

11

To make apple wings as a garnish, halve an apple and lay it cut side down. Make 2 diagonal cuts and lift out a small wedge from the top. Continue to cut, following the lines of the first cut, until 2 wedges remain. Reshape the apple, then gently separate the slices to form a wing shape.

Marinated Pork

4 pork chops
1 onion, finely chopped
½ tsp dried sage
½ tsp dried thyme
1 cup (250 ml) dry cider
2 tbsp oil
1 tbsp butter

1 cup (100 g) all-purpose flour
salt and pepper
2 apples, peeled, cored
  and sliced
¾ cup (175 ml) chicken stock
1 tsp honey
1 tsp Dijon mustard

Marinating meat in oil, cider or wine before cooking tenderizes it, while the herbs add extra flavor. Cover the meat and leave it in a cool place for at least 2 hours or overnight if possible.

Marinate the chops with the onion, herbs and cider for at least 2 hours, turning occasionally.

Heat the oil and butter. Drain the chops and strain the marinade. Season the flour and use to dust the chops, then brown them in the hot butter and oil. Spread the apples in an oiled ovenproof dish and place the chops on top. Fry the strained onion for 5 minutes until soft. Stir in the remaining flour and cook until just browned, then stir in the marinade, stock, honey and mustard. Bring to a boil then pour over the chops. Cover and cook in a preheated oven at 350° F (180° C) for 45 minutes. Serve with mashed potatoes and peas.

15

19

Serve beans or pulses as vegetables with grilled meats to provide healthy and colorful side dishes.

16

To save time, use canned beans, draining and rinsing them well before adding them to the recipe.

20

17

21

18

Dried beans and pulses should be soaked overnight in cold water, then drained and rinsed thoroughly. To cook them, cover with fresh water, bring to a boil and simmer for about 1 hour or until tender.

Quick Goulash

1 onion, finely chopped
1 clove garlic, crushed
1 carrot, diced
2 zucchini, diced
2 tbsp olive oil
1 tbsp paprika
a pinch of freshly grated
    nutmeg
2 tbsp chopped fresh parsley

1 tbsp tomato paste
14 oz (400 g) canned
    tomatoes
3 cups cooked or drained,
    canned red and white
    kidney beans
⅔ cup (150 ml) tomato juice
salt and pepper
2 tbsp sour cream or
    plain yogurt

You can choose almost any type of beans for this dish: black, black-eyed, cannellini, flageolet, lima or soy beans. The recipe also tastes good with lentils or chickpeas. Use a selection to give a variety of tastes and a wonderful range of colors.

Fry the onion, garlic, carrot and zucchini in the oil for 5 minutes until soft. Stir in the paprika, nutmeg, parsley and tomato paste and cook for 1 minute. Stir in the tomatoes, beans, tomato juice and seasonings, cover and cook for 15 minutes. Transfer to a warmed serving dish and drizzle sour cream or yogurt on top. Serve with warm crusty bread and a salad of watercress and cabbage.

22

For a moist result, poach chicken halves covered in water or stock with a few vegetables for about 1½ hours.

26

23

27

Fill tiny bottled peppers with a stuffing of minced meats and herbs, and deep-fry for a delicious hot appetizer or snack.

24

28

25

You can also make shrimp or crab nuggets using finely chopped shrimp or crab claws instead of chicken. Leave out the chili if you do not like things too spicy, or substitute ¼ of a green or red pepper, finely chopped.

Chicken Nuggets

1 lb (450 g) cooked chicken, minced
2 cups (175 g) dry breadcrumbs
1 tbsp butter
2 tbsp all-purpose flour
⅔ cup (150 ml) milk
2 eggs, beaten

½ red or green chili, seeded and chopped
1 green onion, chopped
1 tbsp chopped fresh parsley
salt and pepper
oil for deep-frying

You can either dip the chicken balls into the egg and turn with a fork, or brush them lightly with the egg using a pastry brush. If you have pressed the ingredients together well when you prepared them, they should not break up.

Mix together the chicken and half the breadcrumbs. Melt the butter, stir in half the flour and cook for 1 minute. Gradually stir in the milk and bring to a boil to make a thick white sauce. Stir in the chicken and breadcrumbs with the chili, onion, parsley and seasonings and leave to cool.

Shape the mixture into 1 in (2.5 cm balls) with floured hands. Coat with beaten egg and roll in remaining breadcrumbs. Deep-fry in hot oil for about 5 minutes until golden brown. Drain on paper towels and sprinkle lightly with salt before serving.

Nuggets made with chicken or fish can be served cold as a cocktail snack, or hot with vegetables for supper.

29

31

Make sure you wash leeks thoroughly before slicing to remove any grit which may be lodged between the layers.

30

Use whatever shellfish you prefer for this recipe, but do make sure you buy them live and fresh and use them quickly. Whatever you choose - clams, mussels, scallops - scrub them well and soak them in several changes of fresh water. Discard any which do not close when tapped or do not open during cooking.

If you buy live lobster, cook it with the other shellfish until it turns red, then remove and prepare it. Otherwise, use cooked lobster, fresh or frozen. Halve it lengthwise, cut off the tail and remove the meat. Crack the claws and remove the meat as whole as possible. Discard the head. Buy raw shrimp, if possible, for the sweetest flavor, but cooked shrimp will also be delicious.

Fish Stock

1 lb (450 g) fish bones,
*   skin and heads*
7 cups (1.75 l) water
1 onion, sliced
1 carrot, sliced

1 bay leaf
6 black peppercorns
1 blade mace
1 sprig fresh thyme
1 slice lemon

Bring all the stock ingredients to a boil, then simmer for 20 minutes. Strain the stock and discard the fish and vegetables.

Bouillabaisse

1 carrot, sliced
2 leeks, sliced
1 clove garlic, crushed
6 tbsp (75 g) butter
a pinch of saffron
½ cup (125 ml) dry white wine
1 recipe fish stock
8 oz (225 g) canned tomatoes
1 lb (450 g) cod or halibut fillets

1 lb (450 g) mussels, scrubbed
1 lb (450 g) small clams,
*   scrubbed*
8 small new potatoes, scrubbed
1 lobster, cooked and prepared
½ lb (225 g) large peeled
*   shrimp*
1 tbsp chopped fresh parsley

Fry the carrot, leeks and garlic in the butter for 5 minutes until soft. Add the saffron and wine and simmer for 5 minutes. Add the stock with the remaining ingredients, except the lobster, shrimp and parsley. Bring to a boil, then simmer for about 15 minutes until the shellfish have opened and the potatoes are tender. Add the lobster and shrimp, remove from the heat, cover and let stand for 5 minutes. Sprinkle with parsley and serve with garlic bread and a glass of lightly chilled dry white wine.

21

February

'The Summer hath his joys,
and Winter his delights,
Though Love and all his pleasures are but toys,
They shorten tedious nights.'
Thomas Campion

Spring may be just around
the corner, but still it snows and dismal weather can
make the shortest month seem like the longest.
Brighten the chilly days with fish pies, roasts and
warming casseroles. And forget the cold at
least for the 14th, when you can let the romantic
in you run wild!

FEBRUARY

1

2

3 Finish a Chinese meal with a glass of jasmine tea, which you can buy in many supermarkets or delicatessens.

4

5 Chinese shrimp crackers, fried briefly in hot oil, make a tasty cocktail snack or a good side dish for a Chinese meal.

6

7

Remove the hard central core from tomatoes with a sharp knife, and cut them into wedges. Do not add them to the wok until the last minute so that they retain their shape and a slight crispness. Chinese snow peas and mushrooms also go well with this sauce, with or without peppers.

Cantonese Beef

4 tbsp dark soy sauce
1 tbsp cornstarch
1 tbsp sherry
1 tsp sugar
1 lb (450 g) round or rump
   steak, cut in thin strips
2 large tomatoes

2 tbsp salted black beans
2 tbsp water
1 green pepper
4 tbsp oil
¾ cup (175 ml) beef stock
pepper

Salted black beans are available from specialty stores. Crush the beans in a small bowl with the back of a spoon to make a thick paste. It adds a wonderful authentic flavor.

Mix together the soy sauce, cornstarch, sherry and sugar. Add the meat and set aside. Core the tomatoes and cut them in wedges. Crush the beans to a paste with the water. Cut the green pepper into chunks. Heat the oil in a wok and stir-fry the pepper for 2 minutes, then remove. Add the meat and marinade, and stir-fry for 2 minutes. Add the bean paste and stock, bring to a boil and simmer for 5 minutes until slightly thickened. Add the peppers and tomatoes, season and stir-fry for 1 minute. Serve immediately with boiled rice.

25

FEBRUARY

8

12

9

13 Fold puréed canned peaches into whipped cream with a touch of cinnamon. Chill and serve with ginger snaps.

10 Wash and dry some rose petals. Dip in beaten egg white then in fine sugar, and leave to dry. Use to decorate special desserts.

14 St Valentine's Day

11

To make the raspberry sauce, purée 8 oz (225 g) fresh or frozen raspberries, then rub them through a sieve to remove the seeds. Stir in ¼ cup (25 g) icing sugar to sweeten. This is delicious with the Valentine Creams, poured over ice cream or swirled into yogurt.

Valentine Creams

8 oz (225 g) cream cheese
1⅔ cups (400 ml) whipping cream
¾ cup (75 g) icing sugar
2 tsp ground cinnamon

Whisk the cream cheese together with 4 tbsp of cream until light and fluffy. Sift in the icing sugar and the cinnamon and blend well. Whip the remaining cream until stiff and fold it into the mixture. Line 4 molds with damp cheesecloth, spoon in the mixture and press down to remove any air bubbles. Fold the cheesecloth over the top and stand on a rack over a tray. Refrigerate for at least 8 hours. Turn out carefully, unwrap, and garnish with raspberry sauce and candied rose petals.

Use molds with small holes in the base so that any excess liquid can drain away during chilling. Line the molds with dampened cheesecloth or J-cloth, extending the material beyond the edges of the molds.

27

FEBRUARY

15

19

16

20

If you have time, prepare and cook curries in advance and reheat them. The flavor will be improved.

17

An onion and tomato salad tastes good with Indian foods. Slice onions thinly and mix with thin tomato wedges.

21

18

Spices are used in Indian food to benefit the digestion as well as provide flavor and color. Cook them before adding other ingredients to avoid a harsh taste. Peel ginger root before grating; do not use ground ginger. Wash your hands after preparing chilies as they contain an irritant.

Vegetable Curry

1 onion, finely chopped
1 green chili pepper, seeded and finely chopped
1 small piece ginger root, grated
2 cloves garlic, crushed
1 tbsp oil
½ tsp ground cumin
½ tsp ground turmeric
2 potatoes, diced

1 eggplant, cubed
14 oz (400 g) canned tomatoes, drained
8 oz (225 g) cauliflower florets
⅔ cup (150 ml) vegetable stock
8 oz (225 g) okra
4 oz (100 g) roasted, unsalted cashew nuts
2 oz (50 g) desiccated coconut
salt and pepper
4 tbsp plain yogurt

Fry the onion, chili, ginger and garlic in the oil for 5 minutes until soft. Stir in the spices and fry for 1 minute. Stir in the potatoes, eggplant and tomatoes, cover and cook for 10 minutes until the vegetables are almost tender. Add the cauliflower, stock and okra, cover and cook for 5 minutes until the vegetables are tender. Add the cashews, coconut and seasoning, heat through, then transfer to a warmed serving dish. Drizzle the yogurt over the top and serve with plain rice.

You can use any of your favorite vegetables for this delicious curry. Try it with sliced zucchini, peas, carrots or broccoli. Remember to add first those vegetables that need the longest cooking, so they are all done at the same time.

FEBRUARY

22

Basil has a strong flavor, so don't use too much. If you do not have fresh basil, stir in a little pesto sauce.

26

23

27

Most of the fat in chicken is contained in the skin, so remove this before or after cooking for a healthier meal.

24

28/29

25

Use a very sharp knife to peel limes, lemons or oranges so you can remove all the white pith, which can be very bitter. Remove the pithy center and push out any seeds. Slice as thinly as possible, retaining the shape of the fruit.

Lime-Roasted Chicken

4 chicken breasts
salt and pepper
4 limes
2 tsp white wine vinegar

5 tbsp olive oil
2 tsp chopped fresh basil
1 sprig fresh basil

Rub the chicken with salt and pepper, place in an ovenproof dish and set aside. Use a lemon zester to pare away thin strips of rind from 2 limes, then cut them in half and squeeze the juice. Mix the lime juice and rind with the wine vinegar and 4 tbsp of oil, pour over the chicken, cover and refrigerate for at least 4 hours, overnight if possible, basting occasionally.

Baste the chicken thoroughly, then bake in a preheated oven at 375°F (190°C) for 30 minutes until tender. Meanwhile, peel and slice the remaining limes.

Heat the remaining oil and fry the lime slices and basil for 1 minute until beginning to soften. Arrange the chicken on a warmed serving platter with the lime slices, pour the sauce over, and garnish with the basil sprig. Serve with creamed potatoes and steamed snow peas lightly tossed in butter.

Vary the recipe using lemons and thyme instead of lime and basil for a slightly sharper taste. Always make sure chicken is thoroughly cooked by spearing the thickest part with a skewer. If the juices run clear, the chicken is ready.

31

March

'When daffodils begin to peer,
With heigh! the doxy, over the dale,
Why, then comes in the sweet o' the year;
For the red blood reigns in the winter's pale.'
William Shakespeare

THE WINDS may still be strong and the rain squally, but they toss the yellow heads of the daffodils and scatter the now-green grass with early blossom. The new life of spring begins to burst on every side. Days grow longer as summer approaches. New life is breathing in the kitchen, too, with the early vegetables of the season, crisp and tender, ready for lighter dishes to come.

MARCH

1

Leeks make a nice side dish. Slice them into rings, fry them in a little butter and chicken stock and serve with grilled lamb chops.

5

2

6

Make Breton crêpes with buckwheat flour and serve them with a ham and cheese filling and a mug of dry cider.

3

7

4

Crêpes can be filled with almost anything you like, then rolled up and baked or simply served as they are for a perfect snack, lunch or dessert. Try cottage cheese and walnuts, mushrooms in sauce, shrimp, cooked smoked haddock with chopped tomato and onions, or cherries with sour cream.

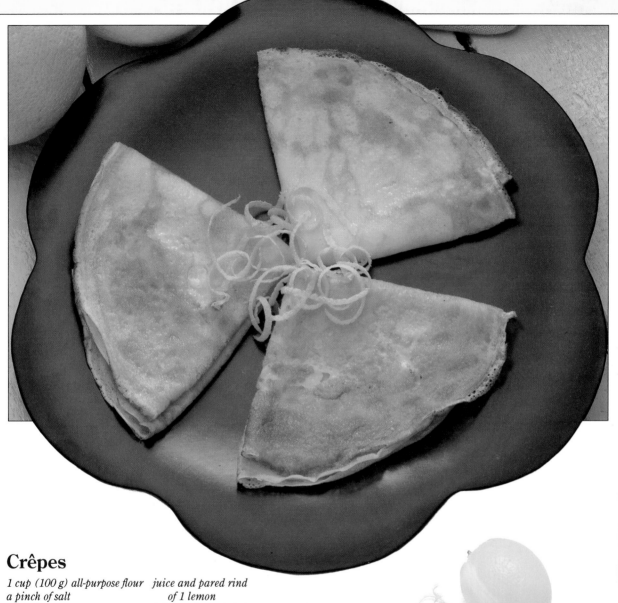

Crêpes

1 cup (100 g) all-purpose flour
a pinch of salt
1 egg, beaten
1¼ cups (300 ml) milk
1 tbsp vegetable oil

juice and pared rind
   of 1 lemon
juice and pared rind
   of 1 orange

Mix the flour and salt and make a well in the center. Beat the egg and milk and stir it into the flour, then beat to a smooth batter. Heat a little oil in a crêpe pan and pour in some batter, tilting the pan so that the batter spreads as thinly as possible. Cook until brown on the base, then turn and cook the other side. Layer the crêpes between sheets of waxed paper and keep them warm while you fry the remaining batter. Garnish with the citrus rind and serve with the juice.

The best way to pare thin strips from citrus fruits is to use a lemon zester; otherwise use a very sharp knife and cut the rind into strips. Make sure you cut off any white pith, which tends to be bitter.

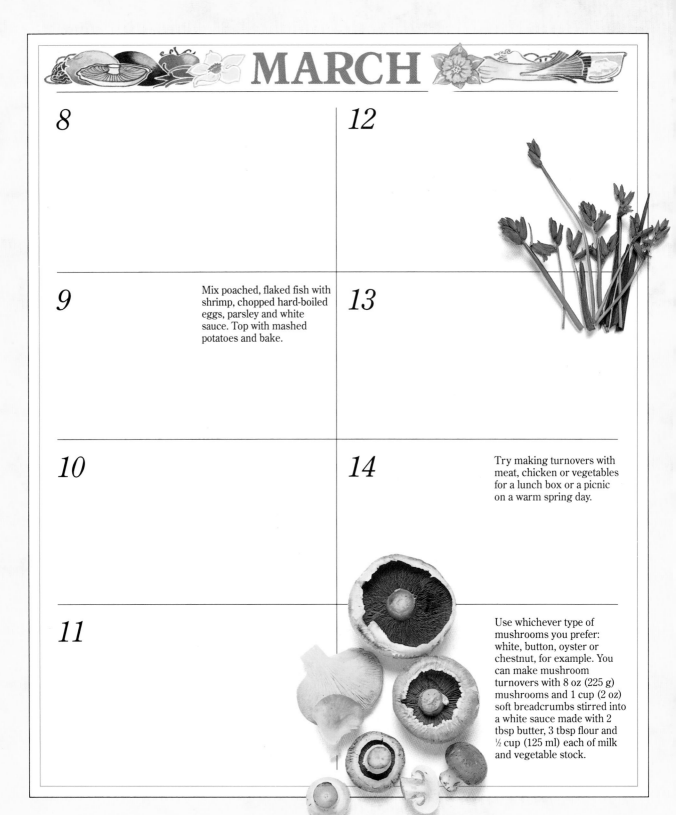

MARCH

8

9
Mix poached, flaked fish with shrimp, chopped hard-boiled eggs, parsley and white sauce. Top with mashed potatoes and bake.

10

11

12

13

14
Try making turnovers with meat, chicken or vegetables for a lunch box or a picnic on a warm spring day.

Use whichever type of mushrooms you prefer: white, button, oyster or chestnut, for example. You can make mushroom turnovers with 8 oz (225 g) mushrooms and 1 cup (2 oz) soft breadcrumbs stirred into a white sauce made with 2 tbsp butter, 3 tbsp flour and ½ cup (125 ml) each of milk and vegetable stock.

Sole Turnovers

4 sole fillets, skinned
salt and pepper
6 tbsp milk
¼ lb (100 g) mushrooms, sliced
2 tbsp butter
juice of 1 lemon

3 tbsp coarsely ground
  hazelnuts
12 oz (375 g) frozen
  puff pastry
1 egg, beaten
1 tsp poppy seeds

Season the sole, roll up and secure with toothpicks. Place in an ovenproof dish with the milk, cover and poach in a preheated oven at 350°F (180°C) for 10 minutes. Drain, remove the toothpicks and leave to cool. Cook the mushrooms, butter and lemon juice in a small pan for about 5 minutes. Let cool, then stir in the hazelnuts. Roll out the pastry, and cut into 4 6-in (15 cm) circles. Place a fish roll on each one and divide the stuffing mixture between them. Brush the edges of the pastry with beaten egg and pinch the edges to seal. Brush all over with egg and sprinkle with poppy seeds. Bake the turnovers on a greased baking sheet in a preheated oven at 400°F (200°C) for 25 minutes until puffed and golden. Serve with a green salad and potatoes glazed in butter.

To seal a turnover, make sure you have brushed the edges well with beaten egg.

Pull the pastry edges up and over the filling and pinch the edges together firmly.

15 Smother slices of braising steak with sliced onions and a little stock, cover and braise in a low oven for 2 hours.

19

16

20 Mix 1½ lb (750 g) ground steak with 1 egg, 2 cups (4 oz) soft breadcrumbs, 1 chopped onion and seasonings to make tasty meatballs.

17 St Patrick's Day

21

18 To make Irish Griddle Scones, knead together 1 cup (100 g) self-raising flour, ½ tsp salt, 3 tbsp (40 g) butter, ½ tsp freshly grated nutmeg, 1 egg and 6 tbsp milk. Make into 2 flat rounds ½ in (1 cm) thick, cut into 6 triangles and cook on a greased heavy pan for about 5 minutes on each side.

Traditionally drunk with oysters fresh from the sea, Guinness beer is synonymous with Ireland, and they say that nowhere but in Ireland does it taste exactly as it should. It gives a wonderful rich flavor and tenderizes meat during the long, slow cooking.

Beef in Guinness

1½ lb (750 g) chuck steak   salt and pepper
½ lb (225 g) carrots   ½ tsp chopped fresh basil
3 tbsp oil   ⅔ cup (150 ml) Guinness
2 onions, chopped   1 tsp honey
3 tbsp all-purpose flour   ⅔ cup (150 ml) beef stock

Cut the steak into about 12 1-inch (2.5 cm) thick pieces. Trim the carrots into pieces about the size of your little finger. Heat the oil and fry the onions for 5 minutes until soft, then use a slotted spoon to transfer them to a shallow greased ovenproof dish. Season the flour, dip in the meat, then fry in the oil until browned. Transfer meat to the casserole with the carrots. Stir the flour into the pan and cook for 1 minute. Stir in the basil and Guinness, bring to a boil and simmer for 1 minute. Stir in the honey and stock, return to the boil and pour over the meat. Cover and bake in a preheated oven at 325°F (160°C) for 1½ hours. Serve with mashed or boiled potatoes and steamed cabbage.

22

Dip onion rings into a thick flour and water batter, fry until crisp and serve with grilled meat and ratatouille.

26

23

27

24

Garlic is very popular in Mediterranean cooking. It gives a wonderful flavor and is also very good for you.

28

25

Eggplants contain bitter juices which should be extracted before you use them. You can either halve them and score the flesh, or slice them thickly. Sprinkle generously with salt and stand them in a colander so that the juices can drain off. Rinse well under running water and pat dry before use.

Ratatouille

2 eggplants
salt
4 tbsp olive oil
2 Spanish onions,
    thinly sliced
4 zucchini, sliced
1 green pepper, chopped

1 red pepper, chopped
2 tbsp chopped fresh basil
1 large clove garlic, chopped
26 oz (800 g) canned
    tomatoes
pepper
⅔ cup (150 ml) dry white wine

Halve the eggplants and score the cut sides diagonally
with a sharp knife. Sprinkle with salt and leave to stand
for 30 minutes. Rinse and pat dry, then chop roughly.
Heat the oil and fry the onions for 5 minutes until
soft and beginning to brown. Stir in the zucchini
and peppers and cook gently for 5 minutes.
Remove from the pan and set aside. Add
the eggplants to the pan and cook for
8 minutes until beginning to brown,
then add the other vegetables and all
the remaining ingredients except the
wine to the pan. Bring to a boil,
then simmer for 15 minutes until
thickened. Add the wine and cook
for a further 15 minutes. Serve hot
or cold.

To prepare peppers, halve
them and remove the seeds
and white pith, then chop
or slice the flesh as
required. Onions need to
be peeled and halved, then
sliced with a sharp knife.
Wash the zucchini, trim the
ends and slice neatly into
rings.

MARCH

29

31

30

To skin tomatoes, cut a small cross into the skins and plunge them into boiling water for 10 seconds, then into cold water. The skins should peel away easily with a sharp knife.

Indian basmati rice has an excellent flavor and stays moist and separate. If you substitute it for long-grain rice, reduce the amount of liquid. You can buy ground saffron or saffron strands. Crush saffron strands in a little boiling water before adding them to the dish.

Saffron Chicken

2 tbsp olive oil
1 small chicken, cut up
salt and pepper
1 onion, finely chopped
1 clove garlic, crushed
2 tsp paprika
8 tomatoes, skinned and
    chopped

1¾ cups (300 g) long-grain rice
3½ cups (900 ml) boiling water
a large pinch of saffron
    strands or ¼ tsp ground
    saffron
1 cup (175 g) frozen peas
2 tbsp chopped fresh parsley

If you are starting with a whole chicken, cut it up before you start the recipe. Cut the chicken in half lengthways down the breastbone and through the backbone. Cut the halves in half again, slitting between the leg joint diagonally up and around the breast joint. Cut away the drumsticks from the leg thigh joint and the wings from the breast joint to make 8 pieces. Remove the skin by pulling and cutting with a sharp knife.

Heat the oil in a large flameproof casserole dish and fry the chicken pieces for about 5 minutes until browned. Season, remove from the dish, and set aside. Add the onion and garlic to the dish and fry gently for 5 minutes until soft but not browned. Stir in the paprika and fry for 30 seconds. Add the tomatoes and cook for 10 minutes until slightly thickened. Stir in the rice, water, saffron and chicken. Bring to a boil, then cover and simmer gently for about 15 minutes. Add the peas and parsley and simmer for a further 5 minutes until the rice is tender and the liquid has been absorbed.

April

'When well-apparelled April on the heel
Of limping Winter treads.'
William Shakespeare

S PRING is here at last!
Refreshed by April showers, the garden begins to
blossom and new plants appear almost daily. April has
a wonderful variety – the weather ranges from cold
and blowy to almost summery and mild. In the
kitchen, too, cooks offer warming fish dishes on
colder days, then tempt you into summer with the
earliest vegetables and salad greens.

1   **April Fool's Day**   The oldest April fool breakfast is the empty egg shell upside down in its cup and beautifully served with hot toast.

5

2

6   Toss lightly steamed broccoli in 2 tsp olive oil and 2 tsp anchovy paste until hot for an unusual side dish.

3

7

4   Make chili flowers from small green or red chilis to decorate oriental dishes. Slit the chilis lengthwise from the tip, leaving about 1 in (2.5 cm) of the stalk end intact. Scrape out the seeds and ribs. Stand the chilis in a bowl of ice water for 1 hour until they curl into flowers.

Spicy Noodles

12 dried Chinese mushrooms
8 oz (225 g) Chinese egg
noodles
5 tbsp oil
4 carrots, thinly sliced
8 oz (225 g) broccoli florets
1 clove garlic

4 green onions, diagonally
sliced
1 tsp chili sauce
4 tbsp soy sauce
4 tbsp rice wine or dry sherry
2 tsp cornstarch

Soak the mushrooms in warm water for about 30 minutes. Meanwhile, cook the noodles in boiling salted water for about 4-5 minutes. Drain, rinse under hot water and drain again. Toss with 1 tbsp of oil. Blanch the carrots and broccoli in boiling water for 2 minutes. Drain and rinse under cold water. Drain the mushrooms, discard the stems and slice the caps. Heat the remaining oil with the garlic in a wok, then remove the garlic. Add the carrots and broccoli and stir-fry for 1 minute. Add the mushrooms and green onions and stir-fry for 2 minutes. Mix together the chili sauce, soy sauce, wine or sherry and cornstarch. Pour over the vegetables and stir-fry until the sauce clears. Add the noodles and toss together until heated through.

You can use any type of egg noodles for this dish, or use rice noodles. Both are available dried in various thicknesses. In China, noodles are a symbol of longevity and are often served at birthday parties as a wish for long life.

APRIL

8

For a tasty buffet dish, purée some light pâté and whipped cream until smooth and pipe it into little rolls of ham.

12

9

13

To make sweet eggs, color tiny pieces of almond paste with food coloring and roll in mixed spice for a speckled effect.

10

14

11

Stuffed eggs make a perfect starter, snack or canapé. They are delicious served cold, so make an attractive dish for a picnic or buffet table. You do not have to stick to hen's eggs. Quail, duck and goose eggs work equally well.

Stuffed Eggs

4 eggs
8 oz (225 g) cooked ham,
    ground
4 tbsp grated mild cheese
4 tbsp sour cream
2 tsp mustard

salt and pepper
2 tsp chopped fresh dill
    or chives
3 tbsp breadcrumbs
2 tbsp butter, melted
1 sprig parsley

Pierce a small hole in the large end of each egg shell and
lower the eggs gently into boiling water. As the water
returns to the boil, roll the eggs around for 2 minutes to
help set the yolks. Cook for a further 8 minutes. Drain, then
set in cold water until ready to shell. Shell the eggs, halve
them lengthwise and remove the yolks. Mash the yolks with
the remaining ingredients except the breadcrumbs, butter
and parsley. Pipe or spoon the mixture back into the whites.
Sprinkle the breadcrumbs on top, and drizzle with melted
butter. Place under preheated broiler for about 3 minutes
until crisp and golden brown. Serve garnished with parsley.

APRIL

15

19

16

Brush a whole, cleaned fish with oil, season with dried oregano and bake at 350°F (180°C) for 10 minutes per inch (2.5 cm) of thickness.

20

Scatter cubes of your favorite hard cheese over a layer of tomato slices and dress with olive oil and pepper.

17

21

18

There are many different varieties of lettuce now available, from the familiar iceberg and Romaine to the more unusual curly endive, radicchio and lamb's lettuce. Try a selection to find your favorites. Darker-leaved varieties tend to be slightly bitter, so use them sparingly.

Spring Salad

14 oz (400 g) cottage cheese
1 carrot, coarsely grated
8 radishes, coarsely grated
2 green onions, thinly sliced
    crosswise
salt and pepper

1 tsp chopped fresh dill or
    marjoram
⅔ cup (150 ml) sour cream
    or thick yogurt
selection of lettuce leaves
4 sprigs fresh dill

Strain excess liquid from the cottage cheese while you
prepare the vegetables. Mix together all the other
ingredients except the lettuce and dill sprigs, and chill for
about 20 minutes. To serve, arrange a selection of lettuce
leaves and a mound of salad on individual plates and garnish
with sprigs of dill. Serve with thinly sliced rye, wholewheat
or French bread and butter.

Grate the vegetables on the coarse
side of the grater to make short
strips which will absorb the
flavors of the salad while
retaining their crispness.
If you are making a large
quantity, it may be
quicker to use a food
processor.

22

23

24

Fry diced leftover lamb in butter with chopped bacon, onion, parsley, diced cooked potatoes and Worcestershire sauce. Top with fried eggs.

25

26

Scoop out the insides of baked potatoes, mix with butter and beaten egg, and pile the mixture back into the skins. Bake until golden.

27

28

Make another delicious lamb stuffing by frying 1 small chopped onion in a little butter, then mixing it with the grated rind and juice of 1 orange, ¾ cup dry breadcrumbs, ½ cup mixed sultanas, raisins and currants, and a little rosemary and thyme, salt and pepper.

Stuffed Lamb

half breast of lamb
1 onion
salt and pepper
2½ cups (225 g) dry
*   breadcrumbs*
¼ cup (25 g) chopped suet

½ tsp dried marjoram
½ tsp dried thyme
grated rind of ½ lemon
1 egg
1 tbsp all-purpose flour
2 sprigs fresh parsley

Bone the lamb. Place the bones in a saucepan with half the onion and some salt and pepper. Cover with water, bring to a boil, skim, cover and simmer for 30 minutes. Strain and reserve the stock. Finely chop the remaining onion and mix it with the breadcrumbs, suet, herbs, lemon rind, salt, pepper, egg and 2 tbsp of stock. Spread the stuffing over the lamb, roll up and tie firmly with string. Bake in a greased roasting pan in a preheated oven at 400°F (200°C) for 1 hour. Transfer the meat to a warmed serving dish and keep it warm. Drain off any excess fat from the pan, stir in the flour and cook for 1 minute. Stir in 1 cup (250 ml) of stock, bring to a boil, stirring, and boil for 3 minutes. Strain into a gravy boat. Garnish the lamb with parsley and serve with new potatoes and zucchini.

For a deliciously creamy and unusual sauce, use slightly less stock for the gravy and mix in 4 tbsp redcurrant jelly and 4 tbsp cream, seasoning to taste. Slice the lamb, arrange the slices on a warmed serving dish and pour over the sauce to serve.

53

29

30

Salmon steaks make a great meal simply brushed with melted butter and crushed garlic, and grilled until tender.

The best way to cook fresh whole salmon is in a court bouillon. Finely chop 2 carrots, 1 onion, 2 sticks celery and 2 dry shallots and mix with 1 bay leaf, 3 parsley stalks, 2 sprigs fresh thyme, 2 tbsp lemon juice, 1¼ cups (300 ml) dry white wine and 3½ cups (900 ml) water. Cover and simmer for 15 minutes. Meanwhile, cut the fins and gills off the cleaned fish, cut an inverted V into the tail and wash it well. Strain the court bouillon over the fish in a buttered ovenproof fish or fish poacher, cover and poach in a preheated oven at 350°F (180°C) for about 8 minutes per lb (450 g) until the fish flakes when tested with a fork.

Leave to cool in the court bouillon, then remove the fish. Snip the skin just below the head and above the tail and carefully peel off the skin. Snip the backbone below the head and above the tail, then split the fish along the backbone with a sharp knife. Ease the bone out from the back without breaking the fish. Salmon steaks can be poached in the same way.

You can add a little chopped dill to the flan if you wish. An attractive feathery herb, it is often used with fish dishes because of its delicate flavor. Dill seeds are also available but these have a stronger taste.

Salmon Flan

6 oz (175 g) frozen puff pastry   salt and pepper
2 tsp cornstarch   1 tbsp butter (optional)
⅔ cup (150 ml) milk   1 egg, beaten
6 oz (175 g) cooked fresh or   4 sprigs fresh dill
   canned salmon

Roll out the pastry and use it to line an 8 in (20 cm) quiche pan. Mix the cornstarch with a little milk. Bring the remaining milk to a boil, stir in the cornstarch mixture, then return to the pan and cook for 1 minute, stirring constantly. Season with salt and pepper. Mix the butter into the fresh salmon, or drain the canned salmon and flake the fish, removing any bones or skin. Remove the sauce from the heat and beat in the egg, then fold in the salmon and spoon the mixture into the pastry shell. Bake in a preheated oven at 375°F (190°C) for 40 minutes. Serve garnished with dill sprigs, and with a crisp salad and wholewheat bread or baked potatoes and green peas.

May

'And the May month flaps its glad green leaves like wings,
Delicate-filmed as new-spun silk,'
Thomas Hardy

SPRING is flourishing, the
summer buds are shooting up and the first tender young
asparagus brings its delicate flavor into the kitchen.
Lightness and softness are the keynotes: the newest
vegetables are meltingly tender, and summer fruits
are beginning to appear on grocery counters.
Summer is just a step away, and you can pack
away your winter coats.

MAY

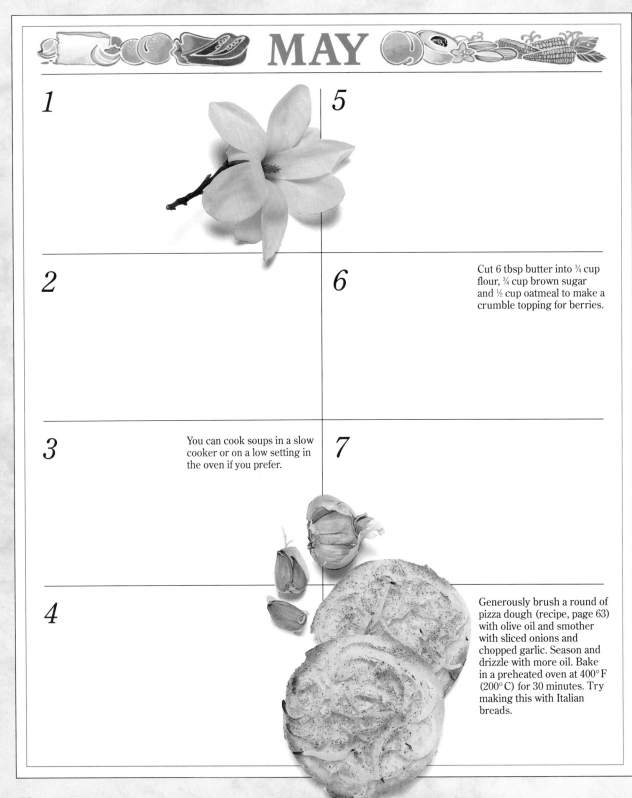

1

5

2

6
Cut 6 tbsp butter into ¾ cup flour, ¾ cup brown sugar and ½ cup oatmeal to make a crumble topping for berries.

3
You can cook soups in a slow cooker or on a low setting in the oven if you prefer.

7

4
Generously brush a round of pizza dough (recipe, page 63) with olive oil and smother with sliced onions and chopped garlic. Season and drizzle with more oil. Bake in a preheated oven at 400°F (200°C) for 30 minutes. Try making this with Italian breads.

Minestrone means 'big soup'. For a thinner soup, omit the pasta and reduce the amount of vegetables.

Minestrone

4 oz (100 g) dried white
    cannellini beans
5 cups (1.2 liters)
    vegetable stock
2 tbsp olive oil
1 onion, finely chopped
1 clove garlic, crushed
1 stick celery, thinly sliced
2 carrots, diced
2 oz (50 g) cut green beans

¼ lb (100 g) greens of
    your choice, shredded
1 zucchini, diced
¼ lb (100 g) tomatoes,
    skinned and diced
1 bay leaf
2 oz (50 g) pasta shells
salt and pepper
1 tbsp chopped fresh basil
2 tbsp chopped fresh parsley

Soak the beans overnight in the stock. Heat the oil and fry the onions and garlic for 5 minutes until soft but not browned. Add the vegetables and fry for 5 minutes until soft. Add the beans and stock, the tomatoes, bay leaf, pasta, salt and pepper. Bring to a boil, cover and simmer for 1 hour until the beans are tender, stirring occasionally. Stir in the basil and parsley and heat through for 5 minutes. Serve with crusty bread.

There are may different recipes for minestrone, but they all make a substantial soup. You can substitute almost any vegetables of your choice, depending on what is available. Any small shape of pasta is fine, or you can use long-grain rice or broken pieces of spaghetti.

MAY

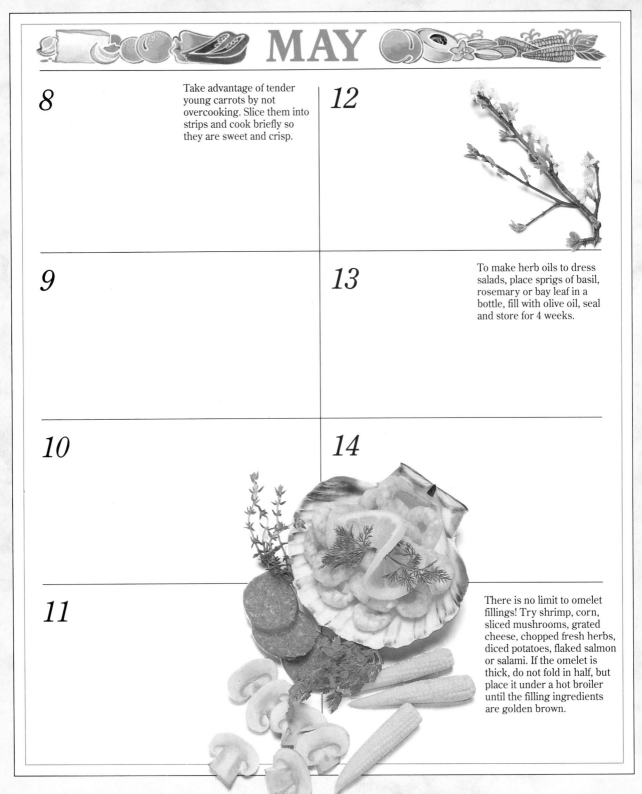

8 Take advantage of tender young carrots by not overcooking. Slice them into strips and cook briefly so they are sweet and crisp.

9

10

11

12

13 To make herb oils to dress salads, place sprigs of basil, rosemary or bay leaf in a bottle, fill with olive oil, seal and store for 4 weeks.

14 There is no limit to omelet fillings! Try shrimp, corn, sliced mushrooms, grated cheese, chopped fresh herbs, diced potatoes, flaked salmon or salami. If the omelet is thick, do not fold in half, but place it under a hot broiler until the filling ingredients are golden brown.

Ham and Pepper Omelet

3 eggs, beaten
2 tbsp milk
salt and pepper
1 tbsp vegetable oil

¼ cup chopped green pepper
2 tomatoes, skinned, seeded
 and chopped
2 oz (50 g) ham, diced

Beat the eggs, milk, salt and pepper. Heat the oil and fry the chopped pepper for 5 minutes until soft. Stir in the tomatoes and ham and heat through for 1 minute. Pour in the egg mixture and stir well until it begins to cook. As the egg begins to set, lift it and tilt the pan to allow the uncooked egg to run underneath. When the underside is cooked and the top is still slightly creamy, fold the omelet in half and serve at once with a crisp salad and crusty bread.

Green and red peppers, zucchini, and any type of ham make excellent additions to omelets. Chop them finely or coarsely, as you prefer, and sauté them until they are just beginning to soften so they still have a slight crunch.

15

To obtain the right temperature of water for yeast, use half boiling water and half cold tap water.

19

16

20

17

Toast pizza toppings on French bread for a quick snack or tasty supper.

21

18

Other good pizza toppings include Italian hams and sausages, tuna, clams, capers, zucchini, olives or Ricotta cheese. To make a calzone, brush the dough with olive oil and cover half with chopped ham, hard-boiled egg, and cubes of Mozzarella. Fold in half, seal and brush with oil before baking.

Pizza Dough

1 tsp dried yeast
½ tsp sugar
¾ cup (175 ml)
   warm water
2 cups (225 g)
   all-purpose flour
a pinch of salt
2 tbsp olive oil

Combine the yeast and sugar in a small bowl, stir in the
warm water and let stand for about 10 minutes until frothy.
Sift the flour and salt into a bowl and make a well in the
center. Add the oil and yeast mixture and work the flour into
the liquid to form a firm dough. Add more flour if necessary.
Turn onto a floured surface and knead until smooth and
elastic. Place in a lightly oiled bowl, cover and let stand in
a warm place for 1 hour until doubled in size. Knead again
and flatten the dough into a 10 in (25 cm) circle.

Italian Pizza

2 tbsp olive oil
1 onion, chopped
1 clove garlic, crushed
14 oz (400 g) canned tomatoes
1 tbsp tomato paste
½ tsp dried oregano
½ tsp chopped fresh basil
1 tsp sugar
salt and pepper

4 oz (100 g) Mozzarella
   cheese, grated
1 oz (25 g) Parmesan
   cheese, grated
½ red pepper, sliced
½ green pepper, sliced
7 black olives, pitted
2 oz (50 g) canned anchovies,
   drained

Heat the oil and fry the onion and garlic for 5 minutes until
soft but not browned. Add the tomatoes with their juice, the
tomato paste, herbs, sugar, salt and pepper. Bring to a boil
and simmer until thick and smooth, stirring occasionally.
Let cool. Spread the sauce over the dough, sprinkle with half
the cheese, then arrange the peppers, olives and anchovies
on top. Sprinkle with the remaining cheese and bake in a
preheated oven at 400° F (200° C) for 20 minutes.

22

When cooking rice, 1 cup of rice cooked in 2 cups of water will serve 3 to 4 people.

26

23

27

24

Soak dried fruits in boiling water for about 10 minutes to plump them up, them drain them well before using.

28

25

As an alternative dressing, whisk together 4 tbsp dry sherry, 3 tbsp olive oil, 2 tbsp white wine vinegar, 1 tsp lemon juice and some salt and pepper. Flavor dressing with a sprinkling of chopped fresh herbs, if you wish.

Rice and Nut Salad

2 tbsp olive oil
2 tbsp lemon juice
salt and pepper
¾ cup (175 ml) golden raisins
⅓ cup (75 ml) currants
¾ cup (175 ml) blanched
   almonds
½ cup (125 ml) cashews
½ cup (125 ml) walnuts

1¼ cups (275 g) brown rice,
   cooked
15 oz (425 g) canned peach
   slices in natural juice
¼ cucumber, chopped
½ cup (100 g) cooked kidney
   beans
6 black olives, pitted

You can substitute apricots
or kiwi fruit for the peaches
if you prefer. Of course,
you can use fresh fruit if
available. Whichever you
choose, this makes a highly
nutritious salad which
is perfect for lunch
or supper.

Put the olive oil, lemon juice, salt and pepper in a screw-top
jar and shake until thickened. Soak and drain the dried
fruits. Chop the nuts. Combine the soaked fruits, nuts, rice,
peaches, cucumbers, beans and olives.
Pour the dressing over and toss
thoroughly. Serve on a bed
of shredded crisp lettuce
or endive.

65

29

31

30

Feta cheese is a soft white Greek cheese made with goats' or ewes' milk. You can substitute a creamy cheese such as Ricotta or any crumbled mild cheese, if you prefer.

To prepare spinach, tear off the stalks by holding the leaves firmly and pulling the stems away. Wash the leaves thoroughly, drain well, then shred with a sharp knife. If you use frozen spinach, simply heat through the thawed spinach with the softened onions, then leave to cool.

You can make a delicious Spinach and Onion Quiche using the same onion and spinach mixture. Line a quiche pan with shortcrust pastry, and cover it with the onion mixture. Beat 3 eggs with 4 tbsp light cream and 4 tbsp milk. Pour the egg mixture over the filling. Season with freshly grated nutmeg and bake in a preheated oven at 400°F (200°C) for 30 minutes.

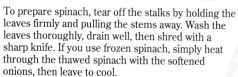

Spinach and Feta Pie

8 oz (225 g) filo pastry
1 lb (450 g) spinach
2 tbsp olive oil
1 onion, finely chopped
1 tbsp chopped fresh dill

3 eggs, beaten
4 oz (100 g) feta cheese
salt and pepper
4 tbsp butter, melted

Filo pastry is available frozen, already rolled into thin sheets. It is easy to handle, but must be kept covered with a damp cloth to keep it moist while you are preparing the dish. Brush lightly with vegetable oil if you prefer it to butter.

Cut the pastry to fit the size of your baking dish, then keep it covered with a damp cloth. Prepare the spinach. Heat the oil and fry the onion for 5 minutes until soft. Add the spinach and stir for 5 minutes over medium heat, then increase the heat to evaporate remaining moisture. Let cool. Mix the dill, eggs, cheese, salt and pepper. Brush the baking dish with melted butter. Brush 8 layers of pastry with butter and lay them in the bottom of the dish. Spread with the filling, then cover with the remaining pastry, brushing each layer with melted butter and scoring the top into diamond shapes. Sprinkle with water and bake in a preheated oven at 375°F (190°C) for 40 minutes until crisp and golden. Let stand for 10 minutes, then cut into wedges and serve with crisp lettuce leaves.

June

'A noise like of a hidden brook,
In the leafy month of June,
That to the sleeping woods all night
Singeth a quiet tune.'
Samuel Taylor Coleridge

EARLY summer – such a
wonderful season as the weather warms, the evenings
grow longer and the color green seems to have more
shades than you could possibly have imagined. Variety
is paramount. You can hardly decide which salad
greens to choose, they all look so delicious. And
at every turn, something new appears in the garden
and in the market. This is a time for experiments –
try them all!

69

JUNE

1

5

Mix ¼ lb (100 g) chopped shrimp, 4 tbsp butter, ½ tsp curry paste and 1 tbsp chopped parsley, spread on toast and broil lightly.

2

Peanut oil is perfect for stir-frying as it has a mild flavor and can be heated to high temperatures.

6

3

7

4

Chinese rice wine is made from glutinous rice, yeast and spring water. It is widely used in China for cooking as well as drinking. You can buy it in specialty shops and Oriental groceries. It should be stored tightly corked at room temperature. You can substitute a dry sherry.

Quick Fried Shrimp

2 lb (900 g) cooked shrimp
2 cloves garlic, crushed
1-inch (2.5 cm) piece fresh
    ginger, finely chopped
1 tbsp chopped fresh coriander

3 tbsp peanut oil
1 tbsp rice wine or dry sherry
2 tbsp light soy sauce
4 green onions, sliced

Shell the shrimp, leaving on the tails. Place them in a bowl with all the remaining ingredients except the green onions, and let marinate for 30 minutes. Heat a wok and add the shrimp and marinade. Stir-fry for a few minutes until heated through, then serve sprinkled with green onion rings.

You can use half shrimp and half shelled scallops for this recipe.

8

9

10

Mix Ricotta cheese with chopped fresh basil and use it to fill pickled cherry peppers. Serve as cocktail nibbles.

11

12

13

Liven up soft ice cream by topping it with fruit purée and sprinkling with chopped nuts.

14

Serve pepper salad with mortadella, prosciutto or salami sausages, crusty bread and dry white wine. Make Pepper and Pasta Salad by frying 2 sliced peppers with 1 sliced onion, 2 sliced zucchini, a clove of garlic and 2 skinned tomatoes. Mix with cooked pasta spirals, season and dress with oil and vinegar.

Pepper Sunburst

2 red peppers
2 green peppers
2 yellow peppers
6 tbsp oil
1 tbsp white wine vinegar
1 small clove garlic, crushed
a pinch of salt

a pinch of cayenne pepper
a pinch of sugar
2 hard-boiled eggs
18 black olives, pitted
1 tbsp chopped fresh
    coriander

You can use any colors of peppers for this salad, and roast them in a hot oven instead of under the broiler. To make the salad in double-quick time, use bottled or canned peppers, drain them thoroughly and slice them into strips.

Halve the peppers and remove the seeds. Press them down to flatten them. Brush the skin side with a little oil and broil until the skins begin to char and split. Place the peppers in a loosely-tied plastic bag and leave for 15 minutes. Whisk together the remaining oil with the wine vinegar, garlic, salt, cayenne pepper and sugar. Cut the eggs into wedges. Remove the peppers from the bag, peel off the skin and cut the flesh into thick strips. Arrange on a serving plate with the eggs and olives. Sprinkle with coriander and spoon on the dressing. Chill for 1 hour before serving.

JUNE

15

Always use freshly grated nutmeg for the best flavor, as this spice deteriorates rapidly once ground.

16

17

18

If you use fresh asparagus, trim them carefully and stand them in boiling water to blanch for a few minutes before using them in the quiche.

19

20

You can freeze partly baked pastry shells so that you can always put together a tasty quiche for supper.

21

Asparagus Quiche

6 tbsp butter
4 tbsp lard
2 cups (225 g) all-purpose
  flour
3 tbsp water
3 eggs
1¼ cups (300 ml) light cream
a pinch of freshly grated
  nutmeg
salt and pepper

2 tbsp all-purpose flour
8 oz (225 g) canned
  asparagus tips
3 oz (75 g) green olives, pitted
1 onion, chopped and fried
  in butter
2 oz (50 g) Cheddar cheese,
  grated
1 tbsp grated Parmesan cheese

Any hard cheese is suitable
in this quiche. Try to buy
fresh Parmesan and grate
it yourself for the best
flavor. Ready-grated
Parmesan does not
taste the same.

Cut 4 tbsp butter and the lard into the flour and mix with
enough water to make a pastry. Roll out and use to line a 10
in (25 cm) quiche pan. Cover with waxed paper and weight
the pastry with dried beans. Bake in a preheated 375°F
(190°C) oven for 10 minutes. Remove the beans and paper.
Whisk the eggs, cream, nutmeg and seasonings. Mix a little
of the mixture with the flour, then stir in the remaining egg
mixture. Arrange the asparagus, olives and onion in the
pastry shell, pour the egg mixture over, and sprinkle on
the cheeses. Dot with the remaining butter and bake for
25 minutes. Reduce the heat to 350°F (180°C) for a further
15 minutes until the quiche is golden.

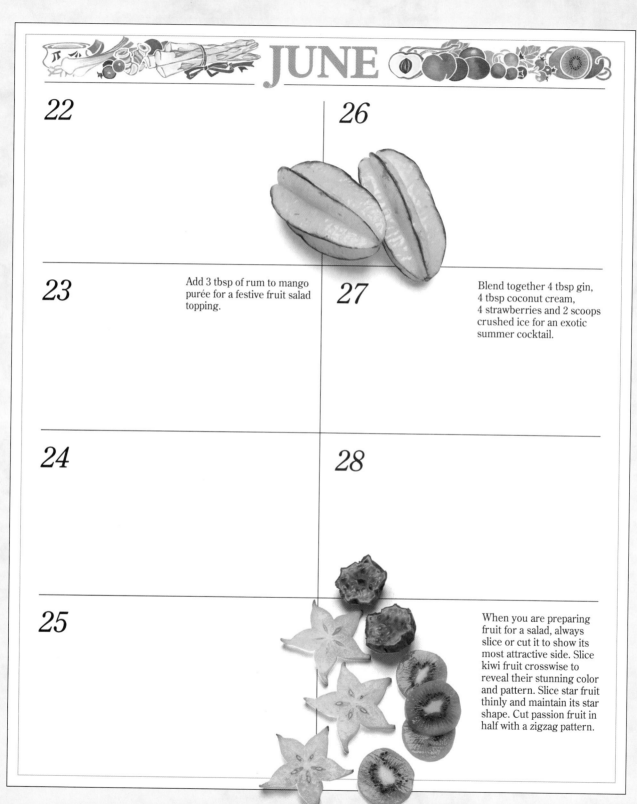

JUNE

22

26

23

Add 3 tbsp of rum to mango purée for a festive fruit salad topping.

27

Blend together 4 tbsp gin, 4 tbsp coconut cream, 4 strawberries and 2 scoops crushed ice for an exotic summer cocktail.

24

28

25

When you are preparing fruit for a salad, always slice or cut it to show its most attractive side. Slice kiwi fruit crosswise to reveal their stunning color and pattern. Slice star fruit thinly and maintain its star shape. Cut passion fruit in half with a zigzag pattern.

Exotic Fruit Salad

3 ripe peaches
3 kiwi fruits
1 star fruit
⅔ cup fresh strawberries

2 ripe mangoes
juice of ½ lime
½ cup red currants
a few strawberry leaves

Raspberries, apricots, cherries, plums, blackberries, grapes, pineapple, passion fruit and guava are all suitable for this wonderful salad.

Plunge the peaches into boiling water for a few seconds, then carefully peel away the skin using a sharp knife. Cut them in half, remove the pits and slice the flesh. Peel and slice the kiwi fruits. Trim and slice the star fruit. Leave the stems on the strawberries and halve them lengthwise. Arrange the fruit on a serving platter. Peel and stone the mangoes, chop the flesh and purée it with the lime juice and half the red currants, then rub the purée through a sieve. Sprinkle the remaining currants over the sliced fruit, pour on the mango purée, garnish with strawberry leaves and chill for at least 1 hour before serving.

77

29

30

Dress cooked diced beets with ½ cup (125 ml) dry sherry, 1 tsp sugar, 1 tbsp wine vinegar, salt and pepper, and chill for 30 minutes.

Another wonderful Mexican dish is Chili con Carne. Cook 2 chopped onions in 3 tbsp oil until soft, then add 1 crushed garlic clove, 2 tsp each ground cumin and paprika and 1 chopped green chili. Cook for 1 minute. Add 1 lb (450 g) ground beef and allow to brown, then stir in 14 oz (400 g) canned tomatoes, 3 tbsp tomato paste, 1 tsp dried oregano, 1 bay leaf and ½ cup (125 ml) beer. Cover and simmer for 1 hour, stirring occasionally. Stir in ½ cup (125 ml) each of drained red and white kidney beans, pinto beans and chick peas. Cook for a further 15 minutes.

Mexican Seviche

1 lb (450 g) cod fillets
juice and grated rind of 2 limes
1 dry shallot, chopped
1 green chili pepper, seeded
   and chopped
1 tsp ground coriander
1 green pepper, sliced
1 red pepper, sliced
1 tbsp chopped fresh parsley
1 tbsp chopped fresh coriander
4 green onions, chopped
2 tbsp olive oil
salt and pepper
1 small lettuce, shredded

Don't be put off by the thought of eating raw fish. The cod will 'cook' in the spicy marinade and the result is absolutely delicious.

Skin the cod and cut it into thin strips across the grain. Place the strips in a bowl and pour on the lime juice. Add the lime rind, shallot, chili, and ground coriander and stir well. Cover and refrigerate for 24 hours, stirring occasionally.

When ready to serve, drain the fish and stir in the peppers, herbs, green onions and oil. Season to taste and serve on a bed of lettuce.

Serve the salad with a bowl of crispy tortilla chips for a wonderful contrast in flavor and texture.

79

July

'I sing of brooks, of blossoms, birds and bowers:
Of April, May, of June, and July-flowers.'
Robert Herrick

HIGH summer – the month
for the soft and melting, richly colored, ripest summer
fruits. Enjoy the warmth of the air, blue skies and
scudding clouds. Unearth the barbecue and picnic
basket and eat outdoors as often as you can, for you'll
have to take your chances when they come. Save
the kitchen for cloudy and showery days, when you
can make jams and pies from the season's
strawberries and raspberries.

JULY

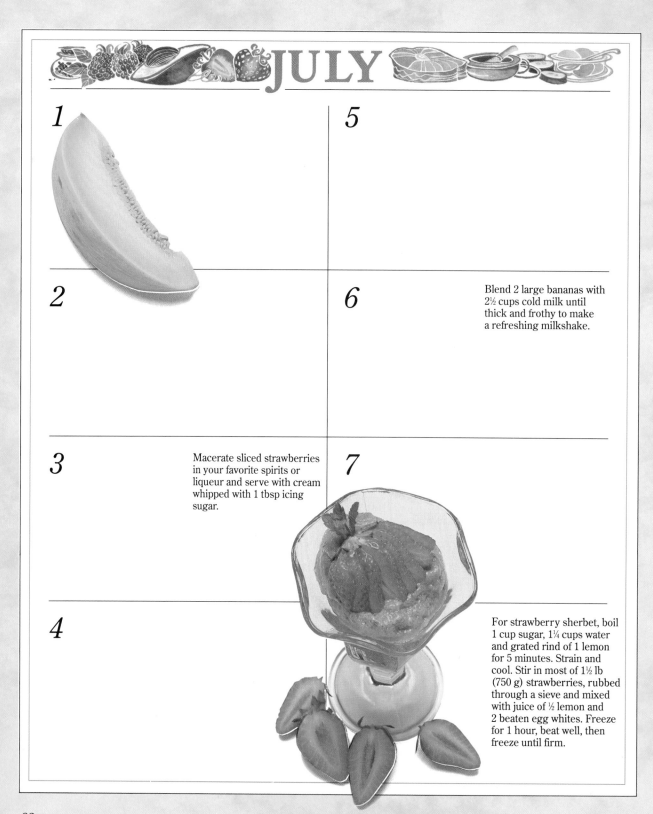

1

2

3

Macerate sliced strawberries in your favorite spirits or liqueur and serve with cream whipped with 1 tbsp icing sugar.

4

5

6

Blend 2 large bananas with 2½ cups cold milk until thick and frothy to make a refreshing milkshake.

7

For strawberry sherbet, boil 1 cup sugar, 1¼ cups water and grated rind of 1 lemon for 5 minutes. Strain and cool. Stir in most of 1½ lb (750 g) strawberries, rubbed through a sieve and mixed with juice of ½ lemon and 2 beaten egg whites. Freeze for 1 hour, beat well, then freeze until firm.

Strawberry Frost

1 lb strawberries, hulled
1 large banana
¾ cup (175 ml) low-fat
   cream cheese

a few drops of vanilla
   essence
1 tsp liquid honey

Put half the strawberries in the refrigerator. Halve or quarter the remaining strawberries, chop the banana coarsely and freeze them together until solid. Just before serving, place the frozen strawberries and bananas in a food processor with the cream cheese, vanilla and honey and process until smooth, pushing the mixture down 2 or 3 times. Divide between individual serving dishes and garnish with the reserved strawberries. Serve at once.

These days, we can buy strawberries almost all the year round, but they are at their best in midsummer when they are ripe, red and juicy with plenty of flavor. For a change, you can make the same recipe using raspberries.

83

JULY

8

Throw a few sprigs of fresh herbs on the barbecue when you are grilling to give simple foods added flavor.

12

9

13

Noisettes of lamb are perfect for the barbecue. They can be marinated in oil and herbs, or just sprinkled with herbs, brushed with oil and grilled.

10

14

11

To make Spiced Tomato Juice, simmer 3 cups (750 ml) tomato juice, ⅔ cup (150 ml) water, 1 tbsp sugar, 1 tbsp lemon juice, 1 tsp Worcestershire sauce, 1 tsp ground cloves, ½ tsp ground cayenne pepper and a pinch of salt for 20 minutes. Strain and chill.

Lamb Kebabs

1½ lb (750 g) lean lamb,
  cubed
juice of 1 lemon
6 tbsp olive oil
1 clove garlic, crushed

1 tbsp chopped fresh oregano
1 tbsp chopped fresh thyme
salt and pepper
12 fresh bay leaves
2 onions, sliced into rings

You can add other vegetables to the kebabs if you wish. Chunks of pepper, mushrooms, onion wedges or zucchini slices are all delicious with lamb.
To prevent wooden skewers from charring during cooking, soak them in water before assembling the kebabs.

Make kebabs with kidneys, fish, chicken, turkey, pork or beef. Choose ingredients which take about the same time to cook.

Place the meat in a bowl. Mix together the lemon juice, oil, garlic, herbs and seasonings, pour over the meat and stir well. Cover and marinate in a cool place for at least 4 hours.

Thread the meat onto skewers, alternating with bay leaves. Slip the onion rings over the meat. Grill under a preheated broiler or on the barbecue for about 10 minutes, turning frequently and basting with marinade. Serve with rice, salad, or grilled peppers.

15

19 For the best flavor, buy free-range or corn-fed chicken. They're worth the slightly higher price.

16 Make a Summer Cocktail with Campari poured over crushed ice in a tall glass and topped with fresh orange juice.

20

17

21

18 To pit an avocado, cut it in half lengthwise and twist the 2 halves apart, then lift out the pit. Always prepare avocado at the last minute and toss it in or brush with lemon juice to prevent it from turning brown.

Chicken and Avocado Salad

8 anchovy fillets
6 tbsp milk
1 green onion, chopped
2 tbsp chopped fresh tarragon
3 tbsp snipped fresh chives
4 tbsp chopped fresh parsley
1¼ cups (300 ml) mayonnaise
2 tbsp tarragon vinegar
⅔ cup (150 ml) plain yogurt
a pinch of sugar
a pinch of cayenne pepper
1 head lettuce, shredded
1 lb (450 g) cooked chicken, diced
1 avocado
1 tbsp lemon juice

Soak the anchovy fillets in milk for 30 minutes, then drain, rinse and pat dry. Purée all the ingredients except the lettuce, chicken, avocado and lemon juice in a food processor. Refrigerate at least 1 hour.

Arrange the lettuce on a serving platter, top with the chicken and spoon on the dressing. Peel, pit and cube the avocado and toss immediately in the lemon juice to prevent discoloration. Sprinkle it over the salad and serve immediately.

This dressing is equally good on a tossed green salad or as a dip for vegetable crudités.

Cut fresh carrots, cucumbers and colored peppers into julienne strips and cauliflower into tiny florets, and arrange attractively around a pot of the dip.

22

23

Fold puréed summer fruits into whipped cream and serve with crisp cookies for a simple summer dessert.

24

25

26

Sliced tomatoes are delicious layered with a sprinkling of sugar. Pour on French dressing and chill for 1 hour.

27

28

A truly unusual Spanish cold soup can be made by grinding 3 oz (75 g) almonds and 1 clove garlic to a fine paste with a little water. Beat in 1½ cups (75 g) fresh breadcrumbs, 6 tbsp olive oil, 1 tbsp sherry vinegar and about 2½ cups (625 ml) water. Season to taste and serve chilled.

As a garnish for the soup, chop 1 onion, ½ cucumber, 3 skinned tomatoes and ½ green pepper. Arrange some of the garnish on top of the soup and offer the rest separately. You can also use croutons, chopped green onions or red onions, or red or yellow peppers.

Gazpacho

1 green pepper, chopped
8 tomatoes, skinned, seeded
  and chopped
1 large cucumber, peeled
  and chopped
1 large onion, chopped
5 oz (150 g) French bread,
  crusts removed

3 tbsp red wine vinegar
3 cups (750 ml) water
salt and pepper
2 cloves garlic, crushed
3 tbsp olive oil
2 tbsp tomato purée
  (optional)

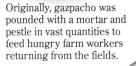

Mix together thoroughly all the vegetables and the bread, breaking it into small pieces by hand. Add the wine vinegar, water, salt, pepper and garlic. Purée the mixture, in batches if necessary, until smooth. Beat in the oil and tomato purée, if using. Cover and chill for at least 2 hours.

Whisk again thoroughly before serving.

Originally, gazpacho was pounded with a mortar and pestle in vast quantities to feed hungry farm workers returning from the fields.

29

30

31

Curries do not necessarily have to be hot. A mild chicken curry made with banana, pineapple or coconut makes a good summer meal.

Try an Indian Carrot and Grape Salad. Cut 3 carrots into julienne strips and mix with ½ lb (225 g) seedless grapes. Mix 2 tbsp oil, 1 tbsp honey, 1 tbsp white wine vinegar, 2 tsp lemon juice, 1 tsp crushed mustard seeds and a pinch of pepper. Toss with the carrots and grapes and sprinkle with paprika.

Fish Curry

½ lb (225 g) salmon fillet
¾ lb (375 g) whitefish fillet
1¼ cups (300 ml) fish or
    chicken stock
salt and pepper
½ cup (125 ml) mayonnaise
1¾ cups (450 ml) plain
    yogurt

2 tsp curry powder
juice and grated rind of ½ lemon
¼ lb (100 g) cooked peeled
    shrimp
1 kiwi fruit, sliced
1 sprig fresh mint
1 tbsp flaked coconut

Place the fish in a shallow pan and just cover with stock. Season to taste and simmer gently for about 15 minutes until the fish is just cooked. Remove the fish from the liquid and let cool slightly. Mix together the mayonnaise, yogurt, curry powder, lemon juice and rind. Flake and debone the fish and mix it into the sauce with the shrimp. Garnish with kiwi fruit, mint and coconut. Serve with boiled rice or new potatoes and a crisp mixed salad.

There are many types of rice available. Brown rice is the unprocessed grain and needs more water and longer cooking.

Long-grain rice grains will stay separate when cooked, perfect for curries and sauces. Risotto rice is a medium-grain, arborio or Italian rice. Short-grain rice goes soft and mushy when cooked, great for puddings.

August

BARBECUE season continues, but the colors of outdoor meals now include the golds and yellows of the early harvests. This is a good time of year to incorporate a few simple dishes from abroad into your cooking repertoire. New and exotic seasonings and flavors will perk up your favorite recipes and enliven your summer table.

93

AUGUST

1

5

2

6

Diced cucumber and melon mixed with shrimp, seasoned and dressed with mayonnaise, make a lovely summer starter.

3

Purée ¾ lb (350 g) cooked carrots, 2 cloves garlic, 1¼ cups (300 ml) yogurt, and ½ tsp each ground coriander and paprika as a tasty dip for raw vegetables.

7

4

Be adventurous when selecting melons. Cantaloupe and honeydew may be the most familiar ones in your grocery store, but a wider variety is now available. You can mix a variety of melons with flesh hues ranging from pink to pale green.

Melon and Prosciutto

1 large ripe honeydew melon   *4 sprigs fresh flat leaf parsley*
16 thin slices prosciutto ham

Halve the melon, and scoop out and discard the seeds and
fibers. Peel off the skin and cut the flesh into 16 thin slices.
Wrap each melon piece in a slice of prosciutto and arrange
on a serving dish. Chill well and garnish with parsley before
serving.

You can serve olives, stuffed
eggs and sliced salami with
this recipe if you wish,
or replace the melon
with fresh figs.

Prosciutto is often known as
Parma ham, but not all
prosciutto comes from
Parma. Wherever it is
made, this type of ham
is rubbed with a mixture
of salt, spices, sugar
and mustard, then
matured to produce
a high quality raw
ham.

95

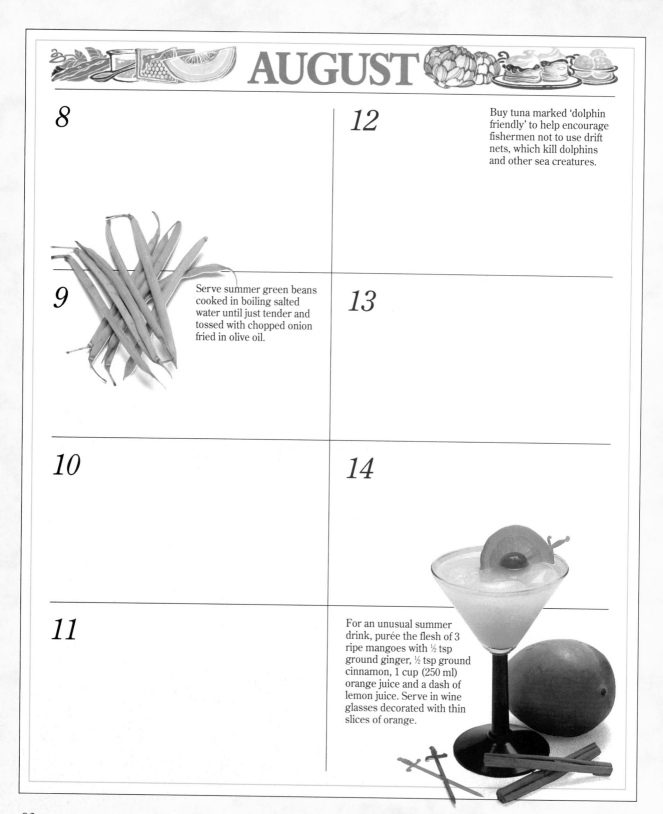

8

12 Buy tuna marked 'dolphin friendly' to help encourage fishermen not to use drift nets, which kill dolphins and other sea creatures.

9 Serve summer green beans cooked in boiling salted water until just tender and tossed with chopped onion fried in olive oil.

13

10

14

11 For an unusual summer drink, purée the flesh of 3 ripe mangoes with ½ tsp ground ginger, ½ tsp ground cinnamon, 1 cup (250 ml) orange juice and a dash of lemon juice. Serve in wine glasses decorated with thin slices of orange.

Salade Niçoise

1 head romaine lettuce
1 hard-boiled egg, quartered
1 tomato, quartered
6 anchovy fillets
10 black olives, pitted
1 tbsp capers
¼ cucumber, diced
1 can tuna fish, drained

4 large artichoke hearts,
    quartered
6 tbsp olive oil
2 tbsp red wine vinegar
½ clove garlic, crushed
1 tsp mustard
1 tsp lemon juice
salt and pepper

Wash the lettuce thoroughly and tear into bite-size pieces.
Toss with the other salad ingredients, taking care not to
break up the eggs. Whisk together the dressing ingredients
and pour over the salad just before serving.

You can use frozen or canned artichoke hearts, or prepare tender fresh ones. Simply cut off the stems, pull the leaves apart and scoop out the hairy choke. Remove the outer leaves down to the tender heart, then cook in boiling water with 1 tbsp lemon juice.

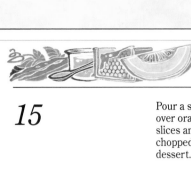 

15

Pour a spoonful of Cointreau over orange and grapefruit slices and garnish with chopped borage for a quick dessert.

19

16

20

Simmer 4 lb (1.75 kg) raspberries until soft and reduced, stir in 4 lb (1.75 kg) sugar, and boil for 20 minutes, then ladle into hot jars.

17

21

18

Make perfect scones using 2 cups (225 g) all-purpose flour, 1 tsp baking powder, 4 tbsp butter, ⅔ cup (150 ml) milk and a pinch of salt. Add 2 oz (50 g) sultana raisins if you like. Roll out, cut into 2 in (5 cm) rounds and bake at 425° F (220°C) for 10 minutes. Serve with butter, homemade jam and thick cream.

Honey-Spice Oranges

1¼ cups (300 ml) clear honey
1¾ cups (450 ml) water
6 sprigs fresh mint
12 cloves
4 large oranges

Bring the honey, water, 2 sprigs of mint and the cloves to a boil in a heavy-bottomed saucepan. Stir until the honey has dissolved, then boil for 5 minutes until syrupy. Let cool, then strain. Pare the rind very thinly from 1 orange and cut it into very fine shreds. Put the shreds into a bowl, cover with boiling water and let stand until cold. Drain well and stir into the syrup. Remove all the skin and pith from the oranges and slice into thin rounds. Arrange on individual plates, pour the chilled syrup on top, and garnish with the remaining mint.

Honey gives sweetness as well as a delicious flavor to the syrup; try using a flower variety for a special taste. The syrup absorbs the flavor of the mint and cloves. Be sure to remove all the white pith from the oranges to eliminate any bitter taste.

 # AUGUST

22

26

23

27

Boil 8 oz (225 g) walnuts for 10 minutes, drain, dry, roll in granulated sugar and dry in a very low oven for 2 hours. Deep-fry until golden, then cool on a wire rack.

24

Dissolve 3 tbsp sugar in 5 tbsp water, pour over 4 peeled, cored and halved pears in a bowl and steam for 20 minutes.

28

25

Chinese dried mushrooms add a distinctive flavor and aroma to Chinese dishes, and they can be used in this recipe instead of the pork. Soak the mushrooms in hot water for about 30 minutes until soft, then squeeze out any excess moisture and remove the tough stems before slicing the caps.

Pork and Shrimp Chow Mein

½ lb (225 g) Chinese noodles
2 tbsp peanut oil
½ lb (225 g) pork fillet, sliced
1 carrot, shredded
1 red pepper, thinly sliced
3 oz (75 g) bean sprouts

2 oz (50 g) snow pea pods
1 tbsp rice wine or dry sherry
2 tbsp soy sauce
¼ lb (100 g) cooked peeled
  shrimp

Cook the noodles in boiling salted water for about
5 minutes, rinse under hot water and drain well. Heat the
oil in a wok and stir-fry the pork for 5 minutes until almost
cooked. Add the carrots and cook for 1 minute. Add the
pepper, bean sprouts, snow peas, wine or sherry and soy
sauce and cook for 2 minutes. Add the noodles and shrimp
and toss over the heat for 2 minutes. Serve immediately.

Stir-fry blanched broccoli florets
in 1 tbsp oil with a small piece of
grated fresh ginger to serve
with this dish.

To grow your own bean sprouts,
wash 4 tbsp dried mung beans,
cover with cool water and soak
overnight. Rinse in cool
water, put them into
a clean glass jar and cover
the top with a piece of
cheesecloth secured
with elastic. Store in a
warm, dark, dry place
for about 4 days, rinsing
the beans 3 times
daily through the
cheesecloth.

 # AUGUST

29

31

Insert a cocktail stick into a thick slice of cucumber. Slice it towards the center, turning the slice as you cut, to make a cucumber spiral garnish.

30

For a Sherry Cobbler, put plenty of crushed ice into a tall glass and half-fill with sherry. Add a splash of Curaçao and a teaspoon of fruit syrup, and stir. Garnish with a sprig of fresh mint and a slice of orange and lemon.

To make a Summertime Soda, mix together the juice of 1 orange, 1 lemon and 1 grapefruit. Pour over ice cubes, top up with soda water to taste and float a scoop of vanilla ice cream on top. Serve with straws and a spoon.

For a refreshing Coconut Cooler for party drivers, mix together 4 cups (1 liter) grapefruit juice, 4 cups (1 liter) pineapple juice and 1 cup (250 ml) coconut cream. Chill well before serving.

Tipsy Cake

14 oz (400 g) canned fruit
    cocktail
5 tbsp sweet sherry
2 oz (50 g) almond cookies
12 slices sponge cake
3 tbsp raspberry jam
2 oz (50 g) slivered almonds

2 tbsp cornstarch
2 tbsp vanilla sugar
1¼ cups (300 ml) milk
1 egg, beaten
1¼ cups (300 ml) whipped
    cream
3 glacé cherries, halved

Drain the fruit. Mix a quarter of the fruit juice with 4 tbsp
sherry. Reserve a few of the cookies for decoration and
crumble the rest. Spread each sponge cake slice with jam
and cut each one diagonally. Arrange one-third of the
sponge cake pieces in a glass bowl. Cover with half the fruit,
sprinkle with half the crumbled cookies and the almonds
and pour over one-third of the juice and sherry mixture.
Repeat the layers of fruit, cookies, nuts and juice,
then top with the remaining sponge cake
pieces and juice.

Dissolve the cornstarch and sugar in a little milk.
Bring the rest of the milk almost to a boil, then stir in the
cornstarch mixture. Bring the mixture to a boil, stirring,
then simmer for 1 minute. Stir in the remaining sherry
and the egg, then cool until lukewarm. Pour over the trifle,
allowing some to trickle down through the layers. Chill,
then decorate with whipped cream, glacé cherries and
the reserved cookies.

You can make your own
vanilla sugar with a vanilla
bean stored in a container
of sugar. Or substitute plain
sugar and ½ tsp vanilla
extract.

September

*'The rule is, jam tomorrow and jam yesterday -
but never jam today.'*
Lewis Carroll

GOLD turns to purple as the
late fruits ripen on the trees and bushes. This is the
month for enjoying the late summer evenings, and for
enjoying plums, pears and apples. Try to find some of
the traditional home-grown varieties produced by
small growers. Steam up your kitchen making jams,
preserves and chutneys for the winter. You might even
revive some old traditions, making pickled onions and
beets for your Christmas table.

1

Toast ⅓ cup (75 ml) raw oatmeal in a heavy pan, stirring until golden. Let cool. Stir in 2½ cups (625 ml) whipped cream, 1 tbsp whisky, and 4 oz (100 g) raspberries. Serve chilled.

5

2

6

3

7

A green salad of watercress, mushrooms and a variety of lettuce leaves contrasts well with rich dishes.

4

You can also make this recipe using peaches or nectarines. Peel and stone the fruit and purée the flesh. Add to the wok instead of the orange rind and juice, and add a squeeze of lemon juice and a little water if the sauce is too thick. Garnish with sprigs of fresh mint.

Duck with Oranges

3 oranges
1 duck
1 tbsp butter
1 tbsp oil
1¼ cups (300 ml) chicken stock
6 tbsp dry red wine
2 tbsp redcurrant jelly
salt and pepper
1 tsp arrowroot
1 tbsp water
1 sprig watercress

Pare the rind thinly off 2 of the oranges and cut into fine shreds. Put the rind in a bowl, cover with boiling water and let cool, then drain. Squeeze the juice from the 2 oranges. Cut away the peel and pith from the remaining orange and slice into thin rounds. Wash and dry the duck.

Heat the butter and oil in a wok and brown the duck all over. Remove the duck from the wok, cool slightly and cut away the leg and wing ends. Cut the duck in half lengthways, then cut each half in 1 in (2.5 cm) strips. Remove the fat from the wok and add the duck pieces. Add the stock, wine, redcurrant jelly, strips of orange rind and orange juice. Bring to a boil and season to taste. Cover and simmer gently for 20 minutes or until cooked. Skim off any fat. Mix the arrowroot and water and stir it into the sauce. Bring back to the boil and simmer for 5 minutes until the sauce is thick. Arrange on a warmed serving dish and garnish with the orange slices and watercress. Serve with roast or Duchesse potatoes and green beans.

Use a sharp knife or poultry shears to cut the duck into strips.

SEPTEMBER

8

9
Boil ⅔ cup (4 oz) sugar and ⅔ cup (150 ml) water, then poach grapefruit slices in it for 6 minutes. Add 4 tbsp brandy and serve hot or cold.

10

11

12
Be careful not to overcook squid, as it will tend to become rubbery.

13

14
Serve squid rings with a selection of dips. Make your own mayonnaise or use a good brand. Flavor individual bowls of mayonnaise with: 1 clove garlic, crushed; 1 tsp curry powder; chopped mixed herbs; or ½ chopped onion, 1 tsp Worcestershire and 2 oz (50 g) crumbled blue cheese.

Crispy Squid Rings

1½ lb (750 g) squid
½ cup (50 g) all-purpose flour
salt and pepper

oil for deep-frying
1 lemon, in wedges
fresh parsley sprigs

Lemon provides a sharp taste contrast to fried foods, especially with fresh parsley or oregano. A mixture of shrimp, scallops and squid rings are exceptionally good cooked this way.

Holding the squid's body, pull away the head. Remove and discard the intestines and plastic-like quill. Remove the skin. Cut the body into rings. Cut the tentacles from the head and separate them. Mix the flour, salt and pepper and toss the squid in the mixture. Heat the oil and fry the squid in batches for about 3 minutes until golden-brown and crisp. Drain on paper towels and sprinkle with salt. Arrange on a warmed serving dish and garnish with lemon wedges and parsley.

15

16

17

Core an apple, slit round the skin to prevent bursting, and stuff with mincemeat. Drizzle with honey and bake at 350°F (180°C) for 1 hour.

18

19

20

Ricotta or Greek yogurt make delicious low-fat alternatives to cream to serve with desserts.

21

You can make an apple purée with any cooking apples. Wash, peel and quarter 1 lb (450 g) apples and simmer them over gentle heat with 3 tbsp water and a little grated lemon peel until soft. Purée in a food processor or rub through a sieve.

Apple and Honey Tart

6 tbsp butter
¾ cup (75 g) wholewheat flour
¾ cup (75 g) all-purpose flour
3 egg yolks
3 tbsp water

1¼ cups (300 ml) apple purée
4 tbsp honey
2 tbsp ground almonds
2 eating apples, thinly sliced

Cut the butter into the 2 types of flour. Beat 1 egg yolk with
2 tbsp water and mix with the flour to make a soft dough,
adding more water if necessary. Roll out and line a 9 in
(23 cm) flan ring. Prick the base with a fork and flute the
edges. Mix the apple purée with 1 tbsp of honey, the
remaining egg yolks and the ground almonds. Spread over
the pastry and arrange the apple slices on top. Bake in a
preheated oven at 375°F (190°C) for 40 minutes.
Warm the remaining honey and brush
over the warm tart.

Brushing the tart with the
honey while it is still warm
gives it a wonderful rich
glaze. You can use honey
glaze on any similar tarts, or
on fruit cakes or
tea breads.

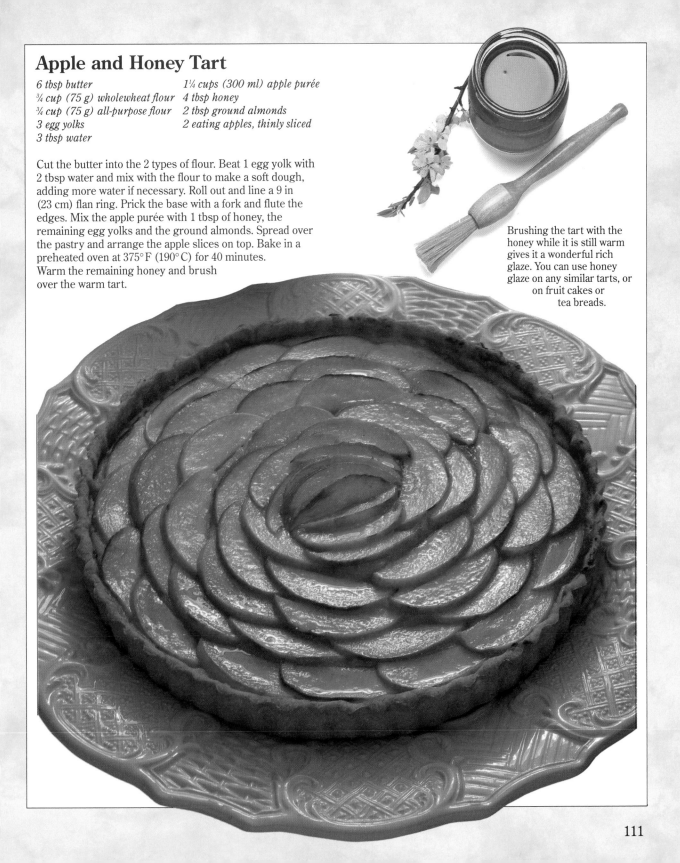

SEPTEMBER

22

Sliced red cabbage steamed with sliced apples is a good accompaniment for rich dishes such as beef or goose.

26

23

27

24

Choose a tasty but light starter – such as deep-fried mushrooms in breadcrumbs or fresh tomato soup – before a strongly flavored meal.

28

25

To make Sauerkraut and Potatoes, boil 1 lb (450 g) sliced potatoes until just tender; do not drain. Fry 2 sliced onions and ¼ lb (100 g) chopped bacon in 2 tbsp oil and add to the potatoes with 1 lb (450 g) sauerkraut. Season and thicken with 1 tbsp cornstarch dissolved in a little cold liquid. Simmer for 30 minutes until thick.

German Pepper Steak

4 x 4 oz (100 g) sirloin or
   rump steaks
2 cloves garlic, crushed
salt and pepper
2 tbsp oil
2 dry shallots, finely chopped
4 tbsp capers
¼ lb (100 g) mushrooms,
   sliced
2 tbsp all-purpose flour
1¼ cups (300 ml) beef stock
1 tbsp Dijon mustard

2 tsp Worcestershire sauce
½ cup (125 ml) dry white wine
2 tsp lemon juice
a pinch of dried thyme
a pinch of dried rosemary
8 baby ears of corn
1 green pepper, sliced
1 red pepper, sliced
2 chili peppers, seeded
   and halved
4 ripe tomatoes, skinned
   and sliced

This is an unusual and tasty recipe which goes well with boiled rice or pan-fried potatoes. You can substitute canned pimento for the fresh red pepper, and add sliced dill pickles along with the tomatoes.

Germans often drink beer rather than wine with meals. Try this dish with a chilled German lager.

Rub the steaks on both sides with garlic, salt and pepper. Heat half the oil in a frying pan and sear the steaks on both sides, then remove them from the pan. Add the remaining oil and fry the shallots, capers and mushrooms for 1 minute. Stir in the flour and cook for 1 minute. Stir in the stock, mustard, Worcestershire sauce, wine, lemon juice, and herbs, and bring to a boil. Add the corn and peppers and return the steaks to the pan. Cook for about 5 minutes or until steaks are done to your taste, then transfer them to a warmed serving dish. Add the chilis and tomatoes to the pan, reheat, and spoon the sauce over the steaks to serve.

29

30

Simmer peeled chestnuts in chicken stock for 30 minutes until tender. Remove the chestnuts, season the sauce with salt and cayenne and boil to reduce by half before pouring over the chestnuts.

To make Damson Plum Chutney, put 3 lb (1.5 kg) pitted damsons, 1 lb (450 g) cored and minced apples, 3 chopped onions, 1 lb (450 g) golden raisins, 1 lb (450 g) each brown and white sugar, 5 cups (1.2 liters) vinegar, 2 tbsp salt, 2 tsp ground ginger, 2 tsp ground cinnamon, and 1 tsp allspice in a large, heavy-bottomed pan. Boil for about 3 hours until thick, stirring frequently. Pour into sterilized jars, seal and label. Store in a cool dry place.

Devilled Cornish Game Hen

4 Cornish game hens
1 tsp paprika
1 tsp dry mustard
1 tsp ground ginger
½ tsp ground turmeric
a pinch of ground allspice
4 tbsp butter, melted
2 tbsp chili sauce

4 sprigs watercress
1 tbsp plum chutney
1 tbsp brown sauce
1 tbsp Worcestershire sauce
1 tbsp soy sauce
a dash of tabasco sauce
3 tbsp chicken stock

Tie the legs of each game hen together and tuck them under the wing tips. Mix together the 5 spices, rub them all over the birds and refrigerate for at least 1 hour. Arrange the hens in a roasting pan and brush with the butter. Roast in a preheated oven at 350° F (180° C) for 20 minutes, basting occasionally. Mix together all the remaining ingredients except the watercress and brush half the mixture over the birds. Cook for a further 40 minutes, brushing with the remaining sauce so that the skins become crisp and brown. Serve garnished with watercress.

Pasta shells go well with this dish. To cook pasta, bring a saucepan of salted water to a boil, add the pasta and stir. Return to the boil and cook just until tender but still slightly firm. Drain well and toss with butter.

October

*'How well I know what I mean to do
When the long, dark autumn evenings come.'*
Robert Browning

AS THE leaves turn and the days grow shorter and colder, the colors of autumn pervade the scene: russet and orange, yellow and gold. The autumn is at its height when the sun shines on a golden October day. Take advantage of the late harvest vegetables, and enjoy hearty meals rich with complex autumnal flavors.

117

OCTOBER

1

2

If you have to keep mussels overnight, wrap them in damp newspaper and keep in the bin at the bottom of the refrigerator.

3

4

5

Make garlic croutons to serve with soup by frying cubes of bread in olive oil with 2 crushed garlic cloves.

6

7

Shrimp are available all year round, either fresh or frozen. Some parts of the world produce particularly large shrimp, often marketed as scampi or langoustines. Two or three of these will suffice for a serving.

Provençale Fish

1 onion, chopped
2 cloves garlic, crushed
3 tbsp olive oil
1½ lb (750 g) tomatoes,
    skinned and chopped
2½ cups (625 ml) dry red wine
2 tbsp tomato paste

salt and pepper
2 lb (900 g) mussels, scrubbed
    and bearded
8 jumbo shrimp
¼ lb (100 g) peeled shrimp
4 crab claws, shelled

Fry the onion and garlic gently in the oil for 5 minutes until
soft but not brown. Add the tomatoes and fry until just soft.
Stir in the wine and tomato paste, season and bring to a boil.
Cover and simmer for 15 minutes. Add the mussels, cover
and simmer for 5 minutes until the mussels have opened.
Discard any that do not open. Stir in the remaining
ingredients and cook, uncovered, for 8 minutes until heated
through.

You can buy crab claws fresh
or frozen. Crack the shells
very carefully with a hammer
or nutcracker and remove
the flesh in one piece,
retaining the shape
of the claws.

119

22

Serve hearty winter dishes with a strong red wine such as a Rioja, and with roast potatoes and a selection of fresh winter vegetables.

23

24

25

26

27

Purée 8 oz (225 g) cooked chickpeas with 1 chopped fried onion, some parsley and 1 egg. Make into patties and fry until golden.

28

Oven-ready frozen pheasants are available all year round. Hen pheasants are usually considered the tastiest and will serve 3 to 4 people; a cock pheasant is slightly larger.

Pheasant in Red Wine

1 tbsp oil
1 tbsp butter
1 large pheasant
2 eating apples, halved
   and cored
1 onion, chopped
1 tbsp all-purpose flour
⅔ cup (150 ml) stock or water

⅔ cup (150 ml) dry red wine
finely pared rind and juice
   of 1 orange
2 tsp brown sugar
salt and pepper
1 bay leaf
1 sprig fresh parsley
1 sprig fresh thyme

Heat the oil and butter in a pan and brown the pheasant all over, then transfer it to a casserole dish with the apples. Fry the onion in the same pan until soft. Stir in the flour and cook for 1 minute. Stir in the stock or water and wine, bring to a boil, stirring, then add the orange juice, rind and sugar. Season with salt and pepper and pour the sauce over the pheasant. Tie the herbs together with kitchen string, add to the casserole, cover and bake in a preheated oven at 350°F (180°C) for 1 hour until tender.

Bouquet garni made with a selection of fresh herbs of your choice will give the casserole a wonderful flavor. If you do not have fresh herbs, make a bouquet garni sachet with dried herbs in cheesecloth. Remember to remove the bouquet garni before serving.

29

31 **Halloween**

30

Shake together a dash of orange bitters, 1 tbsp each fresh orange juice, red vermouth, white vermouth, Grand Marnier and dry gin for a Halloween Cocktail.

Pumpkins make terrific jack-o'-lanterns for Halloween night, but they make an unusual serving dish any night. Try them hollowed out to hold soup, stews, or any savory hot dish.

Pumpkin Soup

3 lb (1.5 kg) pumpkin
4 tbsp butter
1 large onion, sliced
4 cups (1 liter) water
1 cup (250 ml) heavy cream

a pinch of freshly
    grated nutmeg
salt and white pepper
1 tbsp snipped fresh chives

Wash the pumpkin well and cut out the top to make a lid.
Carefully cut most of the pulp off the lid and reserve.
Remove and discard the seeds and fibers. Use a spoon to
scoop out all but 1/2 in (1 cm) of pulp from the interior,
being careful not to pierce through the outer skin. Chop the
pumpkin flesh. Melt the butter and fry the onion gently until
soft but not brown. Add the pumpkin flesh and water, bring
to a boil, cover and simmer gently for 20 minutes. Purée,
return to the pan and add the cream, nutmeg and
seasoning. Reheat and pour into the pumpkin shell.
Garnish with snipped chives.

Use a metal spoon to scoop
out and discard the stringy
pulp and seeds. Carefully
remove the pulp with a
spoon or small knife to
make a shell.

127

November

'No shade, no shine, no butterflies, no bees,
No fruits, no flowers, no leaves, no birds, –
November!'
Thomas Hood

THOUGH the skies can be cold and gray and the landscape takes on the bleak, empty look of winter after the raging beauty of autumn, the warmth of the kitchen can offer winter delights to banish the cold. Nothing warms like a rich soup of fresh root vegetables, sweetened with carrots and parsnips and thickened with barley. And nothing is more cheering than a steaming pudding bulging with dates and dripping with syrup.

1

2

3

Whisk milky hot chocolate in a blender until really frothy, and serve in a tall mug sprinkled with grated chocolate.

4

To make Gingerbread: Mix in a bowl ½ cup (125 ml) molasses, ¾ cup (175 ml) boiling water, 4 tbsp soft butter and ½ tsp baking soda. Sift together ½ cup (100 g) sugar, ¼ tsp salt, ½ tsp ginger, 1 tsp cinnamon, 1½ tsp baking powder, and 1½ cups (175 g) flour. Combine with molasses mixture. Beat in 1 egg. Bake at 350°F (180°C) for 30 minutes.

5

6

Scrub some large potatoes and prick the skins with a fork. Wrap them in foil and bake them in the embers of an autumn bonfire.

7

Spicy Baked Beans

1 lb (450 g) dried flageolet
* or navy beans*
¼ lb (100 g) slab bacon
1 onion

1 tsp mustard powder
6 tbsp black molasses
salt and pepper

Soak the beans overnight in water. Drain, transfer to a saucepan and cover with fresh water. Bring to a boil and boil for 10 minutes. Drain and reserve the water. Place the beans, pork and onion in a large deep casserole dish. Mix together the mustard, molasses, salt and pepper with 1 cup (250 ml) of the bean water and stir it into the beans. Add enough bean liquid to cover the ingredients, exposing only the rind of the bacon. Cover the casserole and bake in a preheated oven at 300°F (150°C) for 2 hours. Stir in the remaining liquid and cook for a further 1½ hours until the beans are tender, uncovering for the last 30 minutes. Remove and discard the onion. Remove the pork, cut off and discard the rind, dice the meat and return it to the dish. Adjust the seasoning and serve with sausages.

Combine ¾ cup (175 g) brown sugar with 1 tbsp butter, ¼ cup (50 ml) corn syrup, 5 tbsp water, and ½ tsp vinegar. Boil to the soft crack stage - 290°F (143°C) on a candy thermometer. Stick apples on wooden skewers, and dip in the hot toffee, then in cold water. Stand on a greased tray. Wrap well if not to be eaten quickly.

NOVEMBER

8

12

Twist bacon slices in a spiral around a skewer, and grill under the broiler until crisp.

9

Serve potato pancakes with several kinds of bacon and a variety of toppings, such as sour cream or blueberry sauce.

13

10

14

11

Serve Mulled Cider hot in mugs. Bring 5 cups (1.2 liters) dry cider to a boil with 4 tbsp brown sugar and a pinch of salt. Tie 4 cloves, a 2 in (5 cm) piece of cinnamon, 4 allspice berries and a strip of orange peel in cheesecloth and add to the pan. Cover and simmer for 15 minutes.

Boxty Pancakes

½ lb (225 g) potatoes, grated
½ lb (225 g) mashed potatoes
2 cups (225 g) all-purpose flour
1 tsp salt
1 tsp baking soda

4 tbsp butter, melted
4 tbsp milk
salt and pepper
2 tbsp oil

Mix the potatoes and mashed potatoes. Mix together the flour, salt and baking soda and stir them into the potatoes. Stir in the melted butter and just enough milk to make the mixture into a batter of dropping consistency. Season with salt and pepper. Heat the oil in a heavy frying pan and fry spoonfuls of the batter until crispy and golden on both sides.

Try a savory version of Potato Pancakes: Mix 1 lb (450 g) grated raw potatoes with 2 chopped onions, 2 oz (50 g) chopped bacon, 1 egg, and ½ cup (50 g) all-purpose flour. Thin the batter with a little milk if necessary and drop into a greased pan. Fry until cooked through and golden on both sides.

133

NOVEMBER

15

Simmer ½ lb (225 g) soaked split peas until tender. Drain and mix with 1 chopped fried onion, 1 egg, salt and pepper. Bake at 350°F (180°C) for 30 minutes.

19

16

20

17

Snow peas and green beans should be cooked just until tender to maintain their flavor and wonderful crisp texture.

21

18

Serve ham with sweet potatoes and okra. Boil scrubbed sweet potatoes in salted water for 25 minutes. Boil okra for 15 minutes, or fry 1 chopped onion and 1 clove garlic in oil, add the okra and fry for 5 minutes. Add 3 tbsp water, ½ tsp turmeric, salt and pepper, cover and simmer for 15 minutes.

Use a small sharp knife to remove the rind from the ham, leaving the fat as smooth as possible. Score the fat in diamond shapes and stud with cloves for added flavor and to enhance the appearance.

You can use ½ cup (125 ml) honey instead of the cola. You can also boil the ham for the first half hour of the cooking time.

Cola Glazed Ham

| 10 lb (4.5 kg) country ham | ½ lb (225 g) dark brown sugar |
| 5 cups (1.2 liters) cola | cloves |

Soak the ham overnight. Place rind side down in a roasting pan, pour over all but 3 tbsp of the cola and bake in a preheated oven at 350°F (180°C) for 2½ hours, basting frequently. Remove the ham from the oven and let cool for 15 minutes. Remove the rind and score the fat to a depth of ¼ in (5 mm). Stick a clove in the center of every other diamond. Mix together the sugar and the remaining cola and spoon over the ham. Raise the oven temperature to 375°F (190°C) and bake for another 25 minutes, basting frequently. Cover loosely with foil if the ham begins to brown too much. Allow to stand for 15 minutes before slicing.

NOVEMBER

22

23

24

Root vegetables such as carrots, beets and parsnips were all common ingredients in 18th century cakes and puddings.

25

Carrot flowers make a colorful garnish. Peel a carrot then cut it into 2 in (5 cm) lengths. Cut v-shapes lengthwise down the carrot and remove the strips. Cut the carrot into thin slices. Arrange to resemble flowers, using caviar or a clove for the center, chive stems and cucumber peel as leaves.

26

27

Fry 3 sliced zucchini and 1 bunch sliced green onions in 1 tbsp each sunflower oil and sesame oil and sprinkle with sesame seeds.

28

Zucchini and Carrot Layer

1 onion, chopped
1 lb (450 g) zucchini, chopped
1 tbsp oil
4 oz (100 g) ground almonds
1 cup (75 g) dry wholewheat
    breadcrumbs
1 tsp vegetable concentrate
1 egg, beaten
1 tsp dried mixed herbs
1 tbsp tomato paste
1 tbsp soy sauce
pepper
1 lb (450 g) cooked, mashed
    carrots
1 sprig fresh rosemary
2 sprigs fresh parsley
1 carrot, cut into strips

Rosemary is a highly aromatic herb which goes well with both vegetables and meats, although it should be used in moderation. This perennial herb, originally from the Mediterranean, is easy to grow in home gardens.

Fry the onion and zucchini in the oil for 5 minutes until soft. Add the remaining ingredients except the carrots, rosemary and parsley, and mix together well. Place half the zucchini mixture in a greased and lined 1 lb (450 g) loaf pan and press down well. Arrange the mashed carrots on top and cover with the remaining zucchini mixture. Cover with foil and bake in a preheated oven at 350°F (180°C) for 1 hour. Allow to cool for 10 minutes before removing from the pan. Garnish with rosemary, parsley and carrot strips.

137

NOVEMBER

29

30

Get ahead for Christmas by making Spiced Cranberry Preserve. Place 1 lb (450 g) cranberries and 1¼ cups (300 ml) cider vinegar in a pan with a ½ in (2 cm) length of cinnamon stick, a ½ in (2 cm) slice of fresh ginger and 1 tsp whole allspice tied in cheesecloth. Bring to a boil and simmer for 25 minutes until the cranberries are soft and the skins pop. Stir in 1 cup (225 g) brown sugar and simmer for 20 minutes. Remove the spices and ladle into hot sterile jars.

Carrots are plentiful in the winter, so make a tasty Carrot Cake. Cream together ½ lb (225 g) butter and 1 cup (225 g) packed brown sugar. Beat in 4 egg yolks, grated rind of ½ orange and 3 tsp lemon juice. Stir in 1½ cups (175 g) self-raising flour, 1 tsp baking powder, 2 oz (50 g) ground almonds, 4 oz (100 g) chopped walnuts and ¾ lb (350 g) grated carrots. Fold in 4 beaten egg whites and spoon into an 8 in (20 cm) greased and lined cake pan. Bake in a preheated oven at 350°F (180°C) for 1½ hours. Beat together 8 oz (225 g) cream cheese with 2 tsp clear honey and 1 tsp lemon juice, spread over the cooled cake and sprinkle with chopped walnuts.

Almond Lattice

6 oz (175 g) frozen puff pastry
¼ lb (100 g) butter
½ cup (100 g) white sugar
2 eggs
1 tsp baking powder
½ tsp almond extract

1 tbsp milk
1 cup (100 g) all-purpose
    flour
4 tbsp damson plum jam
2 oz (50 g) almond paste,
grated

Use two-thirds of the pastry to line a greased 10 in (25 cm)
flan pan. Roll out the remaining pastry and cut into ½ inch
(1 cm) strips. Cream the butter and sugar. Beat in the eggs
one at a time, then the baking powder, almond extract and
milk, adding a little flour between each addition. Fold in
the remaining flour. Spread the jam over the
pastry shell and sprinkle with the almond
paste. Cover with the egg mixture. Make a
lattice on top with the pastry strips, dampen
and crimp the edges, turning in the overlap of
pastry to form a rim. Bake in a preheated oven at
400° F (200° C) for 20 minutes, then at 350° F (180° C)
for another 15 minutes.

This makes a large tart,
but you can reduce the
quantities or make two
smaller tarts and freeze
one. Almonds give this
recipe a distinctive flavor.
If you like a crunchier
topping, sprinkle with
slivered almonds before
putting on the pastry
lattice.

December

'At Christmas play and make good cheer,
For Christmas comes but once a year.'
Thomas Tusser

WHO NEEDS reminding to
enjoy the festive season? December builds to a
wonderful climax when all the planning, preparations
and work reach fulfilment. And so much of that
enjoyment revolves around the kitchen, where
succulent turkey and goose, crisp Brussels sprouts,
sweet parsnips, crunchy and melting potatoes, rich
puddings and elegant pies are prepared, decorated
and brought to the steaming table.

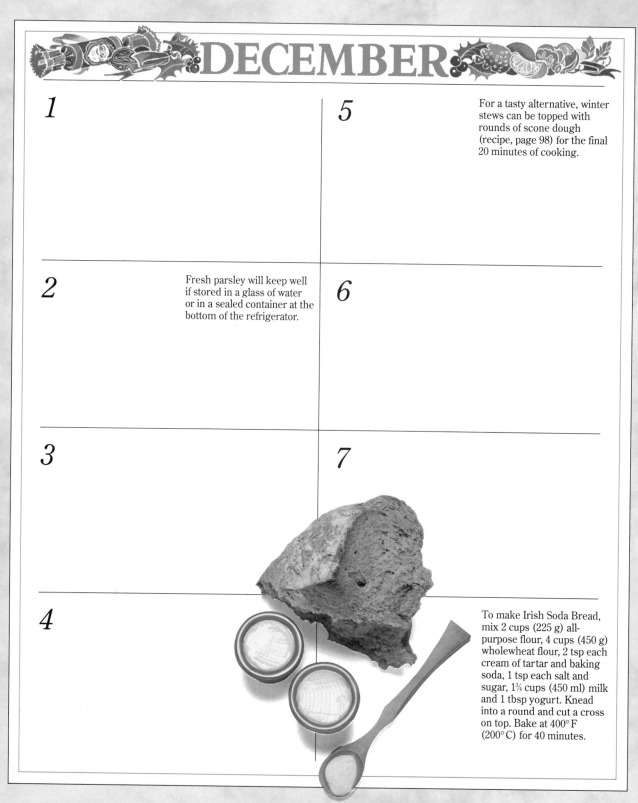

DECEMBER

1

5
For a tasty alternative, winter stews can be topped with rounds of scone dough (recipe, page 98) for the final 20 minutes of cooking.

2
Fresh parsley will keep well if stored in a glass of water or in a sealed container at the bottom of the refrigerator.

6

3

7

4

To make Irish Soda Bread, mix 2 cups (225 g) all-purpose flour, 4 cups (450 g) wholewheat flour, 2 tsp each cream of tartar and baking soda, 1 tsp each salt and sugar, 1¾ cups (450 ml) milk and 1 tbsp yogurt. Knead into a round and cut a cross on top. Bake at 400°F (200°C) for 40 minutes.

Irish Stew

2 lb (900 g) boned lamb, cubed
2 lb (900 g) potatoes, sliced
3 onions, sliced
salt and pepper
2 tbsp chopped fresh parsley
1 tsp chopped fresh thyme
1½ cups (375 ml) water

Trim the meat, leaving on a little of the fat. Season the meat and vegetables with salt, pepper, 2 tsp parsley and the thyme. Layer the potatoes, meat and onions in a large casserole, starting and finishing with a layer of potatoes. Add the water and cover tightly. Cook in a preheated oven at 275°F (140°C) for 2½ hours, shaking occasionally to prevent sticking. Check now and again that the liquid has not dried out. The potatoes will thicken the finished stew so it should not be too runny. Brown the top under the broiler and sprinkle with the remaining parsley.

Slice the potatoes quite thinly for this dish. You will get the best results if you use a mandolin slicer or a food processor, but a sharp knife will also do the trick.

143

DECEMBER

8

For Sweet White Sauce, cook 4 tbsp (50) butter and 2 tsp cornstarch for 1 minute, whisk in 1 tsp sugar, 1¼ cups (300 ml) milk and cook for 3 minutes.

12

9

13

Brussels sprouts are a delicious winter vegetable. Serve them tossed in butter, sprinkled with toasted slivered almonds.

10

14

11

Brandy or Rum Sauce is a must with Christmas pudding. Cream ¼ lb (100 g) butter until soft, then beat in ⅜ cup (75 g) sugar, the grated rind of ½ orange and 3 tbsp of brandy or rum. Chill in small bowls and serve with the pudding or with mincemeat pies.

Christmas Pudding

1 cup (100 g) wholewheat
  flour
1½ tsp baking powder
8 oz (225 g) shredded suet
8 oz (225 g) raisins
4 oz (100 g) sultanas
4 oz (100 g) mixed candied peel

1 oz (25 g) chopped almonds
grated rind of 1 lemon
½ tsp freshly grated nutmeg
2 eggs, beaten
2 tbsp clear honey
⅔ cup (150 ml) milk

Mix together the flour and baking powder. Add the suet,
fruit, peel, almonds, lemon rind and nutmeg. Whisk together
the eggs and honey and mix into the dry ingredients with
the milk. Spoon into a greased pudding basin or heatproof
bowl. Cover with pleated wax paper and secure with string.
Place the bowl in a deep heavy saucepan with
about 1½ in (4 cm) water, cover and
steam for 3 hours, topping up with
boiling water as necessary.
Cool and cover with
clean wax paper,
and store in
a cool dry
place. When
ready to
serve,
steam for
1½ hours.

Made with shortening
instead of suet, this pudding
will delight your vegetarian
guests. Serve with a sweet
dessert wine.

DECEMBER

15

16

17

Make festive garnishes for cookies or cakes with tinted almond paste cut to resemble holly or ivy leaves, Christmas trees or Santas.

18

19

As a contrast to rich traditional desserts, serve simply grilled fish as a main course.

20

21

Make vegetable bundles as an attractive garnish. Trim carrots, zucchini, cucumbers, peppers or celery into matchsticks about 2 in (5 cm) long. Soften strips of green onion in boiling water and use them to tie up the bundles.

Spiced Beef

6 lb (2.75 kg) brisket of beef
1 tsp crushed bay leaf
1 tsp ground mace
1 tsp ground cloves
1 tsp crushed black peppercorns
1 large clove garlic, crushed
1 tsp salt
1 tsp ground allspice
2 tbsp molasses
3 tbsp brown sugar
1 lb (450 g) kosher or
    pickling salt

It takes time for the meat to absorb the spices and flavorings, which tenderize it at the same time as they impart wonderful tastes.

Place the beef in a large glass container. Mix together all the spices and flavorings and rub well into the meat. Cover and refrigerate for 24 hours. Repeat this process every day for a week, turning the meat and rubbing in the spices which will be mixed with the juices drawn from the meat. Tie the meat up firmly in a round and place in a saucepan. Cover with water and simmer gently for 6 hours. Leave in the cooking liquid until cool enough to handle, then place in a dish and cover with a weighted plate. Slice very thinly to serve.

Served cold and thinly sliced, this is a great Christmas dish. It takes a little time, but is not difficult to prepare.

147

DECEMBER

22

Brush squares of filo pastry with melted butter, layer in threes, fill with mincemeat and twist the tops to seal. Bake at 400°F (200°C) for 10 minutes.

24

Christmas Eve

23

25

Christmas Day

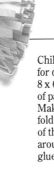

Children can make the frills for dressing a bird. Fold an 8 x 6 in (20 x 15 cm) piece of paper in half lengthwise. Make narrow cuts into the fold to within ¾ in (2 cm) of the edge. Wind the paper around a finger and fix with glue or tape.

To make Sausage Stuffing: Heat 2 tbsp oil and fry ¼ lb (100 g) sausage meat until browned. Add 3 diced sticks celery, 2 chopped onions, 4 oz (100 g) each chopped walnuts and raisins and cook for 5 minutes, stirring. Remove from the heat and drain off the fat. Mix in 1 loaf day-old cubed bread, 1¼ cup (300 ml) chicken stock, 2 tbsp chopped fresh parsley, a pinch each of thyme and sage, salt and pepper.

Apricot and Apple Stuffing goes well with the fattier meat of goose or duck. Cook, drain and chop 6 oz (175 g) dried apricots and reserve the juice. Mix the apricots with 1 tbsp brown sugar, 1 chopped green pepper, 1 chopped cooking apple, 4 chopped celery sticks, 2 cups (100 g) fresh breadcrumbs, 6 tbsp melted butter, grated rind of 1 orange, 2 eggs, salt and pepper. Bind with 5 tbsp apricot juice.

Christmas Turkey

16 lb (7 kg) turkey   *6 tbsp butter*

Use tweezers to remove any feathers on the bird. Remove excess fat inside the cavity. Stuff the cavity of the bird with sausage stuffing, packing in as much as possible. Place some stuffing under the neck flap. Place any remaining stuffing in an oiled casserole and cover. Tie the turkey legs together without crossing them over. Tuck the neck skin under the wing tips and sew up with string. Place the turkey on a rack in a roasting pan and spread some of the butter over the breast and legs. Cover loosely with foil and bake in a preheated oven at 325°F (160°C) for 2½ hours, basting frequently. Remove the foil and continue to roast for a further 2 to 2½ hours until the juices run clear when the thickest part of the thigh is pierced with a skewer. Cook the leftover stuffing for the last 45 minutes of the cooking time. Cover the turkey loosely and let stand for 20 minutes before carving.

26 Boxing Day

30

27 Fry slices of leftover
Christmas pudding in butter,
dust with sugar and serve
with ⅔ cup (150 ml) heavy
cream whipped with 1 tbsp
icing sugar and 2 tbsp port.

31 New Year's Eve

28

To make
Champagne
Cocktails, drop a
lump of sugar into
a Champagne flute
and soak it with
Angostura bitters.
Add a couple of
dashes of brandy and
top with chilled
Champagne. Garnish
with a slice of orange
and a cherry.

29

Spiced Nut Cake

2 cups (225 g) all-purpose
   flour
1 tsp baking powder
1 cup (225 g) sugar
a pinch of salt
a pinch of freshly grated
   nutmeg
a pinch of ground ginger

½ cup (125 ml) orange juice
2 tbsp butter, melted
4 tbsp water
1 egg, beaten
4 oz (100 g) cranberries
4 oz (100 g) hazelnuts,
   chopped
1 tbsp icing sugar

You can replace the
hazelnuts with chopped
walnuts or almonds, and
use multi-colored glacé
cherries instead of the
cranberries.

Sift together the dry ingredients and make a well in the
center. Add the orange juice, butter, water and egg. Beat
until the flour is all incorporated. Stir in the cranberries
and nuts. Grease and line a 9 x 5 in (22 x 12.5 cm) loaf pan.
Spoon in the mixture and bake in a preheated oven at
325°F (160°C) for 1 hour, or until a skewer inserted
in the center comes out clean. Remove from the
pan, peel off the paper and dust with icing
sugar. Slice and serve warm or cold
with butter or cream cheese.

Index of Recipes

Almond Lattice, 139
Almond Soup, 88
Apple, Baked, 110
Apple and Honey Tart, 111
Apple Purée, 110
Apples in Overcoats, 123
Apple Puffs, 122
Apples, Toffee, 131
Apricot and Apple Stuffing, 148
Asparagus Quiche, 75

Banana Milkshake, 82
Batter, 8
Bean Salad, 7
Beans, Spicy Baked, 131
Beef, Cantonese, 25
Beef in Guinness, 39
Beef, Spiced, 147
Beet Salad, Mexican, 78
Berry Crumble, 58
Bouillabaisse, 21
Brandy Sauce, 144
Bread, Basic, 8
Bread, Soda, 142
Broccoli with Anchovy Oil, 46
Broccoli with Ginger, 101
Brussels Sprouts with Nuts, 144

Cabbage, Red, with Apples, 112
Cake, Tipsy, 103
Cakes, Fairy, 9
Campari Cocktail, 86
Carrot Cake, 138
Carrot and Garlic Dip, 94
Carrot and Grape Salad, Indian, 90
Celery, Beefy Fried, 120
Champagne Cocktail, 150
Cheese Fingers, Baked, 9
Chestnuts, 114
Chickpea Patties, 124
Chicken and Avocado Salad, 87
Chicken, Lime-Roasted, 31
Chicken Nuggets, 19
Chicken, Saffron, 43
Chili con Carne, 78
Chocolate Cake, 7
Christmas Pudding, 145
Christmas Pudding, Fried, 150
Cider, Mulled, 132
Coconut Cooler, 102
Corned Beef Fritters, 7
Cornish Game Hens, Devilled, 115
Crab Nuggets, 18
Cranberry Preserve, Spiced, 138
Crêpes, Breton, 35
Cucumber, Melon and Shrimp Salad, 94

Duck with Oranges, 107

Eggs, Stuffed, 49
Eggs, Sweet, 48

Fish and Shrimp Bake, 36
Fish, Baked, 50
Fish Curry, 91
Fish, Provençale, 119

Fish Sticks, 7
Foccacia, 58
French Dressing, 8
Fruit Fool, 88
Fruit Salad, Exotic, 77

Garlic Bread, 120
Garlic Croutons, 118
Gazpacho, 89
Gingerbread, 130
Goulash, Quick, 17
Grapefruit, Poached, 108
Green Beans with Onion, 96

Halloween Cocktail, 126
Ham, Cola Glazed, 135
Ham Crusties, Hot, 9
Herb Oils, 60

Lamb, Irish Stew, 143
Lamb Kebabs, 85
Lamb Noisettes, 84
Lamb, Spiced, 52
Lamb, Stuffed, 53
Leeks, Sautéed, 34

Macaroons, 9
Mango Crush, 96
Mango Rum Topping, 76
Marmalade, 12
Mayonnaise, 8
Meat Kebabs, 85
Meat Turnovers, 36
Meatballs, 38
Melon and Prosciutto, 95
Mincemeat Twists, 148
Minestrone, 59

Noodles, Spicy, 47
Nut Cake, Spiced, 151

Oatmeal Crowdie, 106
Okra, 134
Omelet, Ham and Pepper, 61
Onion Rings, 40
Onion Soup, 13
Onions, Pickled, 120
Orange and Grapefruit Dessert, 98
Oranges, Honey-Spice, 99

Pancakes, 35
Pancakes, Boxty, 133
Pancakes, Potato, 133
Pasta Bowl, 7
Pastry, Shortcrust, 8
Pâté and Ham Rolls, 48
Peach Cream, 26
Pears, Chocolate, 122
Pears, Steamed, 100
Pease Pudding, 134
Pepper and Pasta Salad, 72
Pepper Sunburst, 73
Peppers with Ricotta, 72
Peppers, Tiny Stuffed, 18
Pheasant in Red Wine, 125
Pizza, 63

Plum Chutney, 114
Plum Jam, 114
Pork, Marinated, 15
Pork Chops with Apple, 14
Pork and Shrimp Chow Mein, 101
Potato Soufflé, 52
Potato Surprises, 9
Potatoes, Roasted, 130
Potatoes, Duchesse, 14
Potatoes, Sweet, 134
Pumpkin Soup, 127

Raspberry Jam, 98
Raspberry Sauce, 26
Ratatouille, 41
Rice and Nut Salad, 65
Rum Sauce, 144

Salade Niçoise, 97
Salad, Spring, 51
Salmon Flan, 55
Salmon, Poached, 54
Sauerkraut and Potatoes, 112
Sausage Casserole, 9
Sausage Stuffing, 148
Scones, 98
Scones, Irish Griddle, 38
Seviche, Mexican, 79
Sherry Cobbler, 102
Shrimp Nuggets, 18
Shrimp Parcels, 7
Shrimp, Quick-Fried, 71
Shrimp Toast, 70
Sole Turnovers, 37
Spaghetti, Baked, 121
Spinach and Feta Pie, 67
Spinach and Onion Quiche, 66
Squid Rings, Crispy, 109
Steak, German Pepper, 113
Steak with Onions, 38
Stock, 8
Stock, Fish, 21
Strawberries, Tipsy, 82
Strawberry Frost, 83
Strawberry Sherbet, 82
Stuffing, Fruit, 52
Summer Cocktail, 76
Summertime Soda, 102

Tipsy Cake, 103
Tomato Juice, Spiced, 84
Trifle, Tasty, 7
Tuna Quiche, 7
Turkey, Christmas, 149
Turnovers, 36

Valentine Creams, 27
Vegetable Curry, 29
Vegetable Soup, 12

Walnuts, Chinese Caramel, 100
White Sauce, 8
White Sauce, Sweet, 144

Zucchini and Carrot Layer, 137
Zucchini in Sesame Oil, 136